Julian Assange
In His Own
Words

Julian Assange In His Own Words

COMPILED AND EDITED BY KAREN SHARPE

OR Books

New York · London

© 2021 Karen Sharpe

Published by OR Books, New York and London
Visit our website at www.orbooks.com

All rights information: rights@orbooks.com

First printing 2021

Library of Congress Cataloging-in-Publication Data: A catalog record for
this book is available from the Library of Congress.
British Library Cataloging in Publication Data: A catalog record for this
book is available from the British Library.

Typeset by Lapiz Digital. Printed by BookMobile, USA, and CPI, UK.

paperback ISBN 978-1-68219-263-4 • ebook ISBN 978-1-68219-247-4

CONTENTS

PREFACE

Frank Nicholson, librarian of the University of Edinburgh in 1917, recalled his friendship with a young British officer that autumn: "He was one of those to whom the miseries of the world are misery and will not let them rest, and he went back to spend his life doing what he could to palliate them." The officer was a twenty-four-year-old second lieutenant undergoing treatment for shell shock at Craiglockhart War Hospital. He was also a poet. His name was Wilfred Owen. Owen recovered and returned to the war to palliate the misery of the men under his command. His empathy for suffering humanity extended to enemies, who shared the same brutal experiences. He studied German under Nicholson to build friendships after the war. His death from German machine-gun fire four days before the Great War ended on November 11, 1918, made that impossible. Owen, whose great poems "Dulce et Decorum Est" and "Anthem for Doomed Youth" consecrate the sacrifices of the First World War, resembles no one in our time as much as Julian Assange.

Like Owen, Assange has taken the side of the victims against the powerful who conspire against them in secret. Like Owen, Assange has paid a price in mental anguish. He may also, like Owen, pay with his life if his persecution is prolonged. British Magistrate Vanessa Baraitser's decision of 4 January this year to deny the American application for Assange's extradition to the United States is, for the moment, a stay of execution. The British authorities, rather than release him, returned him to his cell in in the notorious Belmarsh Maximum Security Prison to await the government's appeal. If a higher court reverses Baraitser's verdict, Assange will proceed to the United States for a trial on 18 criminal charges, most under the draconian 1917 Espionage Act, and a maximum sentence of 175 years. If the court upholds her judgement, Assange may at last go free. The process may last a year. Meanwhile, he must endure the same terrible conditions that have reduced his health to the extent that Magistrate Baraitser did not believe he would survive more punitive confinement in the United States.

Whichever way it goes, the message is clear: do not mess with the national security state. Its reach is long, and its fist is hard. It is safer for journalists to write about fashionable clothing, fast cars, gourmet food, and other commodities, including celebrities, that provide an advertising-friendly environment. Don't pry. Tell whistleblowers to keep their documents and conceal criminality. Don't bother the public with unpleasant facts. After all, "All's best in this, the best of all possible worlds." Those who don't accept that can swallow Purdue Pharma's OxyContin until they do. That's what it's for.

In these pages, you will read Julian Assange's words as he wrote or spoke them. They carry the authority of the victim's advocate who risked his freedom for them and forfeited his liberty and his health. "We do not have national security concerns," he says. "We have concerns about human beings." So did Owen, who wrote in the preface to a book of poems he did not live to see published, "My subject is War and the pity of War. The poetry is in the pity."

Assange's subject too is war, what the American–Israeli writer and dissident Jeff Halper called "the war against the people" in his book of that name. No one reading the military cables made public by WikiLeaks, with their casual dismissal of civilian deaths and torture, can avoid pity for war's victims. Assange, like Halper, has provided documentary evidence of the expansion of surveillance and control of ordinary citizens' lives mirroring the Israeli security establishment's domination of Palestinians under military occupation. Not only Palestine, but much of the world, is a gigantic laboratory to test equipment, techniques, psychological manipulation, and violence to prevent people from protesting their powerlessness and impoverishment. How else could humanity accept that 1 percent of the population hoards 88 percent of the wealth while the poorest half makes do with 1 percent?

This book serves as a corrective to the disinformation surrounding Julian Assange and WikiLeaks. When the U.S. Army Counterintelligence Center initiated what it called a program to "damage or destroy this center of gravity" called WikiLeaks in 2008, the psychological warfare against Assange began. Other U.S. agencies—the Pentagon, the Central Intelligence Agency, the National Security Agency, and the State Department— followed the Army's lead in investigating, surveilling, and defaming Assange. The resources mobilized against a lone publisher and journalist were unprecedented, a tribute to Assange's impact. So many lies have circulated that the public has not had the chance to know what Assange has actually done and said. Now, it does.

Charles Glass, 2021

ACKNOWLEDGMENTS

First and foremost, I must thank Julian Assange for the world-changing information and revelations he has uncovered and published at great personal peril, and for his wisdom and courage that inspire so many of us to question and work for change. Much gratitude goes to OR Books, for including this book among the many excellent ones they publish, with special thanks to Catherine Cumming, whose careful reading assured the factual and stylistic accuracy of the text. Immeasurable gratitude to Mark Powelson, for the astute and invaluable advice he provided throughout the process. Much appreciation to Joe Lauria, who offered initial suggestions and facilitated important connections. And deep thanks to people who provided greatly appreciated suggestions and offered ongoing encouragement: Henriette Chardak, Viktor Dedaj, Ulysse Diaz, Diana Johnstone, Alexandra Lefebvre, Annie McStravick, Susan Moldow, Aisha Sharpe, and Zoe Sharpe. And enormous appreciation to all those journalists, authors, and filmmakers from whose works many of the quotations in this book were taken, among whom: Decca Aitkenhead, Tariq Ali, Chris Anderson, Nikki Barrowclough, Al Burke, Carole Cadwalladr, Steve Croft, Suelette Dreyfus, Andrew Fowler, John Goetz, Amy Goodman, Oscar Grenfell, Megyn Kelly, Raffi Khatchadourian, Margaret Kunstler, Clara López Rubio, Stefania Maurizi, Simon Murphy, Juan Pancorbo, Hans Ulrich Obrist, John Pilger, Afshin Rattansi, Darius Rochebin, Marcel Rosenbach, Martin Smith, Michael Sontheimer, Yanis Varoufakis, and Slavoj Žižek. And of course grateful acknowledgment to the millions of people all over the world who continue to demand that Julian be freed and that freedom of speech prevail so that publishers and journalists like Julian may speak freely, holding power accountable.

INTRODUCTION

Who am I? I fought for liberty and was deprived of all liberty. I fought for freedom of speech and was denied all speech. I fought for the truth and became the subject of a thousand lies.[1]

Award-winning WikiLeaks founder and publisher Julian Assange has effectively been silenced for nearly three years, beginning in 2018 when his Internet access was cut off by the Ecuadorian embassy where he had been granted asylum, and continuing through to today when he is locked away in a British prison.[2]

---

1   Tweet sent by Julian on April 10, 2019, the day before he was hauled out of the Ecuadorian embassy. https://wiseupaction.info/2020/10/17/advocating-for-julian-assange-publisher-of-wikileaks-org-by-maxine-walker/.

2   On April 11, 2019, Julian was illegally dragged from the Ecuadorian embassy in London by British authorities, having sought asylum there on June 19, 2012, and was incarcerated in high-security Belmarsh Prison in Woolwich.

Yet in books, essays, interviews, talks, and documentaries, this erudite, analytic, prophetic voice comes through clearly, reverberating with a force around the world. From Tahrir Square to boardrooms occupied by the 1 percent, from the ruins of Fallujah to the corrupt corridors of Washington, from governmental mouthings by the mainstream media to political leaders violating their peoples' rights, Julian's words have enabled millions to discover—and act upon—hidden truths. And caused others to try to silence and erase them. But while Julian may, for the moment, be silenced, whether by the walls enclosing him or the assaults on his mind through years of isolation considered torture by international legal[3] and medical bodies,[4] his words live on. As reminder, as inspiration, as exhortation.

---

3 On August 17, 2020, a group of 152 distinguished legal experts from around the world, together with 15 lawyers' associations, sent an open letter to the British government documenting numerous flagrant violations of domestic and international laws perpetrated against Julian over the past decade, and demanding that he be immediately released and granted freedom from torture, arbitrary detention, deprivation of liberty, and political persecution. ("Prominent lawyers and legal associations demand Assange's freedom", Oscar Grenfell, World Socialist Web Site, August 17, 2020, https://www.wsws.org/en/articles/2020/08/17/assa-a17.html).

4 In a letter published in the British medical journal the *Lancet* on June 26, 2020, 200 eminent doctors from around the world, representing 216 colleagues from 33 countries, decried yet again

Julian Assange in His Own Words consists wholly of quotes by Julian. Through revealing his philosophy, politics, perspicacity, and humanism, the quotations underscore the critical importance of this man who has done more than anyone to uncover how governments, politicians, corporations, the military, and the press truly operate.

In his writings and talks, in addition to addressing the significance of the information contained in the millions of

the ongoing mistreatment of Julian that they first wrote about on February 17, when they condemned the "torture and medical neglect" that since then, with the coronavirus pandemic, had exacerbated the seriousness of his situation. ("In letter to the Lancet, doctors condemn torture of Assange and demand his release," Oscar Grenfell, World Socialist Web Site, June 26, 2020, https://www.wsws. org/en/articles/2020/06/26/assa-j26.html). When United Nations Special Rapporteur on Torture Nils Melzer, along with two medical doctors, visited Julian in prison in May of 2019, they recognized clear signs of psychological torture and they called for an immediate end to such treatment. "The evidence is overwhelming and clear," Melzer said. "Mr. Assange has been deliberately exposed, for a period of several years, to progressively severe forms of cruel, inhuman or degrading treatment or punishment, the cumulative effects of which can only be described as psychological torture. . . . In 20 years of work with victims of war, violence and political persecution I have never seen a group of democratic States ganging up to deliberately isolate, demonise and abuse a single individual for such a long time and with so little regard for human dignity and the rule of law. . . . The collective persecution of Julian Assange must end here and now!" ("UN expert says 'collective persecution' of Julian Assange must end now," United Nations Human Rights Office of the High Commissioner, May 31, 2019, https://www.ohchr.org/EN/NewsEvents/Pages/ DisplayNews.aspx?NewsID=24665.)

leaked documents published by WikiLeaks, Julian reveals an exceptional breadth of knowledge that ranges from quantum physics to Greek mythology, from macroeconomics to modern literature, from empires of old to empires of today, and of course everything to do with the Internet. In assimilating and interpreting this knowledge he invites us to question further and to use that knowledge to make the world a better place.

Julian's prodigious intelligence and passion can be seen clearly in discussions and debates with others—in the books *Cypherpunks* and *When Google Met WikiLeaks*, for example; in talks at TED, the United Nations, the Oslo Freedom Forum, the European Parliament, the Frontline Club, Oxford University; in exchanges with artist Ai Weiwei, the then-president of Ecuador Rafael Correa, the journalist and filmmaker John Pilger, the director at the London Serpentime Galleries Hans Ulrich Obrist; and in numerous media interviews.

* * *

The trajectory of Julian's life reveals a logical evolution. As a small child, Julian had an overwhelming curiosity about the world around him, with a desire "to overcome barriers to knowing."[5] At age eight he already had a keen interest in philosophy and mathematics, reading dozens of related books.[6] By 11 Julian had mastered the Commodore 64, a very early mass-produced computer, exploring programs and code.[7] By age 15 he was "breaking encryption systems used to keep people from sharing software, and then later breaking systems used to hide information in government computers."[8]

But it wasn't all books and computers. Growing up in rural Australia in the 1970s and early 80s, Julian says he "lived like Tom Sawyer—riding horses, exploring caves, fishing, diving, and riding my motorcycle."[9] The peripatetic existence he, his mother, and his half-brother lived (more than 50 different towns, 37 different schools, he claims),[10] at times by choice, at others to hide from the father of his half-brother, enriched him in immeasurable ways[11] and led easily to his nomadic journey-

---

5   "In Conversation with Julian Assange, Part I," Hans Ulrich Obrist, Journal #25, e-flux, May 2011, https://www.e-flux.com/journal/25/67875/in-conversation-with-julian-assange-part-i/.

6   Andrew Fowler, *The Most Dangerous Man in the World,* Skyhorse Publishing, 2013, p. 4.

7   Ibid., p. 10.

8   Obrist, "In Conversation with Julian Assange, Part I."

9   Ibid.

10 Ibid.

11 Fowler, *The Most Dangerous Man in the World,* p. 15.

ing later on, sleeping on couches all over the world, carrying a backpack filled with phones, cables, and computers. As he explains, "The sense of perspective that interaction with multiple cultures gives you I find to be extremely valuable, because it allows you to see the structure of a country with greater clarity, and gives you a sense of mental independence."[12]

Julian's abhorrence of injustice, which motivates so much of what he does, was apparent when he was quite young. "He always stood up for the underdog," says his stepfather, Brett Assange.[13]

Even at a young age Julian sought like-minded people to work together with him to redress wrongs he saw in the world. In his teens, living in Melbourne, he joined with two other young people to found The International Subversives and published a magazine with the same name. Considering what they were doing "ethical hacking",[14] they were driven by a desire to oppose what they saw as dangerous and wrong, pri-

---

12 "The secret life of WikiLeaks founder Julian Assange," Nikki Barrowclough, *Sydney Morning Herald,* May 22, 2010, https://www.smh.com.au/technology/the-secret-life-of-wikileaks-founder-julian-assange-20100521-w1um.html.

13 Fowler, *The Most Dangerous Man in the World*, p. 4.

14 Ibid., p. 15.

marily nuclear armaments, vowing to do no harm in sites they entered.

As Julian and author Suelette Dreyfus recount in *Underground*,[15] they were able to gain access into places that "read like a Who's Who of the American Military Industrial complex," including the Pentagon, Lockheed Martin, the Stanford Research Institute, NASA, NorTel.[16] They often left little messages so that the hackees might know someone had been there, which of course wrought great havoc. It also resulted in a dogged police officer being put on their tail. Julian was charged three years later, and went to trial two years after that, when the judge fined him A$2,100 in reparations, expressing

---

15 Suelette Dreyfus and Julian Assange, *Underground,* Canongate, 2012. Originally published in Australia in 1997, the book (primarily written by writer and journalist Suelette Dreyfus with research by Julian), recounts the most unusual backgrounds, brazen exploits, dangers encountered, ruses used, solutions invented, pursuits outwitted, of Julian, aka Mendax, and a handful of his hacker collaborators, including Par, Trax, Anthrax, Electron, Wandii, and Prime Suspect. In the Introduction to the book, Julian clarifies the meaning of *hacker*: "people who use technology to solve problems with 'thinking from outside the box,'" adding, it "doesn't imply any illegal activity, but rather simply reflects someone who can find clever technical solutions to hard problems. It is this kernel of unusual creativity, not their illegal activities, that makes the hackers in *Underground* so interesting. This kernel carried through to WikiLeaks." (*Underground,* p. xi).

16 Ibid., p. 293.

his concern that "highly intelligent individuals ought not to behave like this, and I suspect it is only highly intelligent individuals who can do what you did."[17]

Another group of "highly intelligent individuals" Julian joined up with are the Cypherpunks, whose mailing list Julian had contributed to from the beginning in the 1990s.[18] They call for cryptography and similar methods to be used to effect political and societal change around the world. [19] In the Introduction to the eponymously titled book, Julian says that it is not a manifesto but a warning: "The Internet, our greatest tool of emancipation, has been transformed into the most dangerous facilitator of totalitarianism we have ever seen."[20] Julian once again brought together likeminded individuals to draw out their best ideas regarding this threat. "I met with three friends and fellow watchmen on the principle that perhaps in unison our voices can wake up the town," he explains. The resulting discussion is presented in the 2012 book.[21]

---

17   Ibid., p. 360.

18   Julian Assange, with Jacob Appelbaum, Andy Müller-Maguhn, and Jérémie Zimmermann, *Cypherpunks: Freedom and the Future of the Internet*, OR Books, 2012, p. 7.

19   Ibid., p. v.

20   Ibid., p. 1.

21   Ibid., p. 6.

WikiLeaks, which Julian founded in 2006, follows logically from the Cypherpunk movement, building on its traditional juxtaposition of "privacy for the weak, transparency for the powerful"[22] and their method of using "mathematics and programming to create a check on the power of government."[23] As he has described WikiLeaks, it's the "rebel library of Alexandria. It is the single most significant collection of information that doesn't exist elsewhere, in a searchable, accessible, citable form, about how modern institutions actually behave."[24] And the information contained therein has been used, among other things, to win court cases, topple governments, change policies.

In high school Julian was given the moniker "The Prof"[25] because of his "bookish" nature and his eagerness to share his knowledge with his cohorts. WikiLeaks is the culmination of his gathering and sharing of knowledge that can encourage people to make a difference.

---

22 Ibid., p. 7.

23 Obrist, "In Conversation with Julian Assange, Part I."

24 "Assange: Why I Created WikiLeaks' Searchable Database of 30,000 Emails from Clinton's Private Server," Democracy Now interview Part I, July 25, 2016, https://www.democracynow.org/2016/7/25/exclusive_wikileaks_julian_assange_on_releasing.

25 Fowler, *The Most Dangerous Man in the World*, p. 11.

With secure procedures for transmitting material from whistleblowers—Chelsea Manning being the best known—and all those concerned with finding an outlet for the truth, WikiLeaks, as of 2015, had released from among its 10 million documents and associated analyses: the Collateral Murder video, which shocked the world with its graphic recording of the U.S. military massacre of more than 12 civilians (including two Reuters journalists) walking down a residential Baghdad street; the Afghan War Diary containing more than 90,000 precise and often gruesome reports of the U.S. military's deadly actions; the Iraq War Logs consisting of nearly 400,000 US Army field reports that reveal war crimes and the true number of civilians killed; Cablegate, more than 251,000 US diplomatic cables showing numerous consequential scandals around the world; the Guantanamo Files, revealing the routine torture and abuse of prisoners held at Guantanamo Bay; and the Spy Files, showing global mass surveillance. In the next two years WikiLeaks published Hillary Clinton's and the Democratic National Committee's emails showing political corruption; Vault 7, the largest leak of CIA files, and much more.[26]

---

26 Tariq Ali and Margaret Kunstler, editors, *In Defense of Julian Assange*, OR Books, 2019, pp. xxix-xxxii.

Though Julian has often been the face and voice of WikiLeaks,[27] it has been an inclusive, collaborative endeavor. Natália Viana describes how she was one of many young journalists from all over the world invited to Ellingham Hall in Norfolk where Julian was under house arrest (ostensibly for the Swedish sexual assault allegations that were subsequently dropped), to determine how best to release the leaked US embassy cables in their specific regions.[28] For Julian, collaboration is fundamental. "Our organization delegates its excess source material to other journalists who will have more impact and who will do a better job," he explains.[29] "That quest to protect the historical record and enable everyone to be a contributor to the historical record is something that I have been involved in for about 20 years."[30] To Viana, Julian and

---

27 Award-winning Icelandic investigative journalist Kristinn Hrafnsson was WikiLeaks' spokesperson between 2010 and 2017. In September 2018, Julian turned over the editorship to him when his legal battles and increasing persecution prevented him from fulfilling that role (https://www.wsws.org/en/articles/2019/12/03/hraf-d03.html). As Julian has been cut off from contact with the public, Kristinn has spoken on his behalf around the world.

28 Ali and Kunstler, *In Defense of Julian Assange*, p. 335.

29 *60 Minutes Rewind*, interview by Steve Croft, January 30, 2011, https://www.youtube.com/watch?v=Ubknv_CxSUY.

30 Democracy Now at the Frontline Club, August 16, 2012, https://www.democracynow.org/2012/8/16/ from_our_archives_full_video

WikiLeaks are responsible for inaugurating "a new era in journalism, in which news outlets collaborate instead of compete."[31]

Julian is largely self-taught but when he was 32 he embarked on a full-time course (never completed) in math and physics at the University of Melbourne. It was through these studies that he further forged his knowledge of and respect for scientific methods. He often talks about WikiLeaks being based on the notion of "scientific journalism—that things must be precisely cited with the original source, and as much of the information as possible should be put in the public domain so that people can look at it, just like in science, so that you can test to see whether the conclusion follows from the experimental data."[32] This method is what has enabled WikiLeaks to publish an enormous volume of materials with not a single word proven to have been wrong.[33]

_of_wikileaks_julian_assange_philosopher_slavoj_iek_with_amy_goodman.

31   Ali and Kunstler, *In Defense of Julian Assange*, p. 341.

32   Julian Assange, *When Google Met WikiLeaks,* OR Books, 2014, p. 126.

33   "WikiLeaks has been publishing for 10 years. In that 10 years we've published 10 million documents. Several thousand individual publications, several thousand different sources. And we have never got it wrong." From "The Secret World of US Election: Julian Assange talks to John Pilger," Dartmouth Films, November 5, 2016, https://www.youtube.com/watch?v=_sbT3_9dJY4. Nor has it been found

It was perhaps these scientific studies that helped Julian become an adept strategist—for creating and implementing WikiLeaks, for organizing political actions, for preparing legal cases. When his life changed so drastically after being placed under house arrest at Ellingham Hall, his movements limited to daily visits to the local police station, Julian had to come up with a new modus operandi. "WikiLeaks had always been a guerilla publisher," he explains. "We would draw surveillance and censorship in one jurisdiction and redeploy in another, moving across borders like ghosts. But at Ellingham I became an immovable asset under siege. We could no longer choose our battles. Fronts opened up on all sides. I had to learn to think like a general."[34]

Despite mischaracterizations about Julian in much of the media, what comes across so clearly in Julian's writings and actions is his abiding respect for others. This respect is accorded not just to sources whom he fiercely protects and readers whom he feels deserve to be given complete information, including primary sources, but also to victims of US mil-

---

that anyone was ever physically harmed by a WikiLeaks release (see *When Google Met WikiLeaks*, p. 195).

34   Assange, *When Google Met WikiLeaks*, p. 14.

itary atrocities whose names he cites to emphasize that they are humans, not numbers, and even to those with whom he may disagree. And it extends to acknowledging the contributions of others: to those anonymous people who supplied WikiLeaks with information; to supporters who surrounded the Ecuadorian embassy in London to keep the British police from taking him away;[35] to all those who helped WikiLeaks releases to be published around the world; and to the many young people who have been educated by the Internet and are becoming important voices within their organizations.[36] By paying tribute to the contributions of others, Julian deflects attention from his own importance.[37] "I hardly know anyone who says 'I' as reluctantly as Assange," says Angela Richter, a writer and director.[38] Indeed in the many talks, interviews, and

---

35   Official Statement by Julian Assange from the Ecuadorian Embassy, August 19, 2012, https://wikileaks.org/Official-Statement-by-Julian.html.

36   Democracy Now at the Frontline Club.

37   How very different the biased and wholly inappropriate assessment of Julian made by District Judge Michael Snow at the April 11, 2019 hearing at Westminster Magistrates Court: "his behaviour is that of a narcissist who cannot get beyond his own selfish interests" ("Assange branded a 'narcissist' by judge who found him guilty," Simon Murphy, *Guardian*, April 11, 2019, https://www.theguardian.com/media/2019/apr/11/assange-branded-a-narcissist-by-judge-who-found-him-guilty).

38   Ali and Kunstler, *In Defense of Julian Assange*, p. 167.

documentaries I watched in compiling material for this book, it was "we" that prevailed over "I" so many times over.

The "we" in Julian's personal life now includes Stella Moris, one of Julian's lawyers and his fiancée, and their two sons, Gabriel, born in 2017 and Max two years later, fathered when Julian was still in the Ecuadorian embassy. On April 11, 2020, the first year anniversary of Julian's incarceration in Belmarsh Prison, The WikiLeaks Channel released an interview with Stella in which she revealed for the first time her relationship with Julian.[39] Since the announcement, she has been a major spokesperson on Julian's behalf, eloquently pleading for his release because of his deteriorating health inside the prison and the iniquities that put and keep him there.

Challenging governments and powers with WikiLeaks releases, and for those acts enduring more than nine years of incarceration, a number of those wholly cut off from the world, has taken considerable courage on Julian's part. He was aware of the enormous risks he was taking, particularly extradition to the clutches of the U.S. where he would face 17 charges under the 1917 Espionage Act and one for conspiring with hackers to

---

39   "Assange Family", TheWikiLeaksChannel, April 11, 2020, https://
www.youtube.com/watch?v=LgK5ZqjvC5s&feature=youtu.be.

obtain classified information, with a possible sentence of 175 years. In a discussion in the Ecuadorian embassy with Srećko Horvat, author and co-founder of DiEM25, he said, "Yes, the situation is tough, but I'm confident there are prices to pay for what you believe in."[40]

Julian's bravery is infectious. Says Angela Richter, "He often cheered me up with the saying, 'Courage is contagious' . . . he has this effect that encourages you to risk more."[41] And it is this courage—as well as the injustices that Julian and WikiLeaks have revealed—that has encouraged some news organizations to become "braver" and publish, among others, releases from the Afghan War Diary,[42] and spurred on WikiLeaks supporters around the world to protest, publish articles, hold conferences, sign petitions.

John Pilger, who is a friend and an ardent supporter of Julian's, speaks about leaving him after a visit in Belmarsh at the end of November 2019, when he experienced the draconian conditions of the prison and observed the diminished physical

---

40 Ali and Kunstler, *In Defense of Julian Assange*, p. 140.

41 Ibid., p. 167.

42 Obrist, "In Conversation with Julian Assange, Part I."

state of his dear friend. "I looked back, as I always do. Julian sat alone, his fist clenched and held high."[43]

For someone who was widely celebrated as a beacon of freedom of the press (Julian was *Time* magazine's People's Choice Person of the Year in 2010, and the recipient of numerous prestigious journalism and human-rights awards[44]), to suddenly be damned as a pariah following unproven sexual assault allegations—yet remain unbowed—has required enormous courage. For someone who was constantly on the move, from Cairo to California, Tanzania to St. Petersburg, Iceland to Ireland, researching, organizing, speaking, to suddenly have 330 square feet as his personal space[45] inside the small Ecuadorian

---

43 Transcription of the speech John Pilger gave at the Free the Truth conference, St. Pancras New Church, November 28, 2019, https://www.wsws.org/en/articles/2019/11/30/pilg-n30.html.

44 The awards he has received include: The Economist New Media Award (2008), The Amnesty New Media Award (2009), Time Person of the Year, People's Choice (2010), Le Monde Readers' Choice Award for Person of the Year (2010), Sam Adams Award for Integrity (2010), the Martha Gellhorn Prize for Journalism (2011), Sydney Peace Foundation Gold Medal (2011), Catalan Dignity Prize (2019), European United Left-Nordic Green Left Award for Journalists, Whistleblowers and Defenders of the Right to Information (2019), Stuttgart Peace Prize (2020), Gary Webb Freedom of the Press Award (2020), and he has been nominated eight times for the Nobel Peace Prize.

45 "Julian Assange, a Man Without a Country," Raffi Khatchadourian, *The New Yorker*, August 21, 2017, https://www.newyorker.com/

embassy in London[46] and then a cell in Belmarsh under even more confined conditions—yet to remain stalwart—reflects extraordinary resilience.

Such resilience enabled Julian to remain productive even while confined in the Ecuadorian embassy from June 2012 to April 2019, under very difficult circumstances, latterly without, Internet or telephone connections. Julian helped to publish 5 million documents, produced 3 books,[47] launched more than 30 publications, and gave 100 talks.[48] A substantial output even from someone living in complete liberty. When he was

---

magazine/2017/08/21/julian-assange-a-man-without-a-country.

46 "Julian Assange finally leaves his tiny room, but what was it like in there?", Richard Trenholm, c/net, April 11, 2019, https://www.cnet.com/news/julian-assange-finally-leaves-his-tiny-room-but-what-was-it-like-in-there/.
The total space of the embassy is 2,153 square feet, of which Julian had 330 square feet to himself, and access to most of the rest when feasible. Two artists who visited Julian regularly in the embassy in 2013 created a life-sized replica of Julian's living space, complete with papers, books, whiskey glasses, devices, cables, folders, phones, etc., at the FACT art centre in Liverpool that people could enter and get a sense of Julian's cramped, sunless life in the actual embassy. Whether artists' rendering or identical recreation is unclear.

47 Ali and Kunstler, *In Defense of Julian Assange*, p. 167.

48 Ibid., p. 295.

asked during an interview to write a mathematical formula for WikiLeaks, he wrote on a piece of paper, "Publish or Perish."[49]

But there is also a lighter side of Julian evidenced by his ready sense of humor. When asked by Srećko Horvat how he felt about being a character in an Asterix comic,[50] he replied, "It's better than receiving the Nobel. Many more people received the Nobel Prize than became characters in Asterix."[51] Julian has been nominated eight times for the Nobel Peace Prize, and likely prefers to be seen alongside Asterix and his tiny band combatting the Romans than beside such warmongers as Barack Obama, Henry Kissinger, and Menachem Begin, all Nobel Peace Prize laureates.

* * *

---

49 "In Conversation with Julian Assange, Part II," Hans Ulrich Obrist, Journal #26, e-flux, June 2011, https://www.e-flux.com/journal/26/67921/in-conversation-with-julian-assange-part-ii/.

50 *Asterix and the Missing Scroll* (written by Jean-Yves Ferri, drawings by Didier Conrad, Les Éditions Albert René, 2015) about controlling information, in which the character Confoundtheirpolitix is loosely based on Julian. A roving reporter (circa 50 B.C.), Confoundtheirpolitix is perpetually in pursuit of the next hot scoop, investigating all situations in which he finds himself.

51 Ali and Kunstler, *In Defense of Julian Assange*, p. 143.

Julian Assange in His Own Words is far from an exhaustive compilation of Julian's words—there is so much more out there, and, we fervently hope, so much more to come.

This book has no beginning and no end. Like Julio Cortazar's *Hopscotch*, you can read it from the beginning to the end or start anywhere, jump around. You can choose pages randomly. You can follow a particular subject, censorship, for example, or follow a particular year, to have an idea what Julian might have been thinking then. You can go through the book just reading the headings to each quotation—they give an encapsulation.

Julian's writings are often like a ripe fruit that has split open and released its seeds, bursting forth as they do with end notes giving sources, expanded information, commentary, related links. The Prof, so desirous of sharing the vast volume of information he has stored, so determined to respect the reader's need for truth. This book replicates that method to a degree. Many sources are listed here so you can go deeper, ponder how it all resonates for you, what implications you can draw, how you might act upon the information. I'm sure that would please Julian enormously.

How you understand Julian and his observations will come from your interpretation of his words, unfiltered by commentary or critique, though here they are admittedly siphoned selectively from an overwhelming flow. In making the difficult decisions as to what to include and what not, I leave it up to readers to determine if I have followed Julian's prescription for what a book should be: "A book must not be true merely in details. It must be true in feeling. True to the visible and the invisible. A difficult combination."[52]

At the time of writing Julian is still locked away in high-security Belmarsh Prison, although the magistrate Vanessa Baraitser had ruled on January 4, 2021 against extraditing him to the U.S., basing her decision on the inhumane conditions in US supermax prisons that would place Julian at risk of suicide. Although conditions in Belmarsh are not much better, especially during the Covid lockdown, she denied him bail on January 6, insisting he would "abscond" before the appeal hearing and thus deny the prosecution its chance to appeal. Julian's health, both mental and physical, has been continually deteriorating, and because of chronic lung problems, he is at high risk of contracting Covid-19. Despite urgent and increasing pleas from all

52 Dreyfus and Assange, *Underground*, p. xxv.

over the world—from parliamentarians, leading human-rights authorities, medical doctors, religious leaders, artists, legal professionals, journalists, writers—to release Julian, at the very least, to house arrest, Judge Baraitser was intransigent.

On January 15 U.S. prosecutors lodged an appeal contesting Baraitser's decision to block extradition. On July 7 the British High Court agreed to hear the appeal, but on limited grounds. Coincidentally or not, the Court's decision was announced 11 days after the prosecution's case was greatly compromised when its star witness, a diagnosed sociopath convicted of fraud, embezzlement, and crimes against minors, acknowledged (according to an article in the Icelandic bi-weekly *Stundin*), that his testimony incriminating Julian was based on lies, recompensed by a promise from U.S. prosecutors for immunity.[53] With no date set for the appeal hearing, Julian will remain in Belmarsh for several more months, convicted of no crime.

---

53 "Key witness in Assange case admits to lies in indictment," Bjartmar Oddur Þeyr Alexandersson and Gunnar Hrafn Jónsson, *Stundin*, June 26, 2021, https://stundin.is/grein/13627/.

Regardless of the outcome of Julian's legal ordeal, it will never be too late for his words to reverberate far and wide—if not to save his life, then to save ours.

I am unbroken, albeit literally surrounded by murderers, but the days when I could read and speak and organize to defend myself, my ideals, and my people are over until I am free! Everyone else must take my place. [54]

---

54   Julian Assange, letter from prison, published in *The Canary,* May 13, 2019, https://defend.wikileaks.org/2019/05/26/julian-assange-writes-a-letter-from-belmarsh-prison/.

ACCOUNTABILITY

Transparency and accountability are moral issues that must be the essence of public life and journalism.[55]

ACCOUNTABILITY THROUGH PUBLISHING

"We are accountable to the public. . . . All the fruits of our labor are published. We are a publishing organization. There is nothing that we do that does not result in material that is being published. So the public can see what it is we do. We don't do anything that doesn't result in publishing. The public chooses to support us by defending us politically, by giving us money, and by giving us source material. And the media chooses to work with us or not, depending on whether they think we're doing a good job. . . . We survive on a week-to-week and month-to-month basis purely as a result of public donations, purely as a result of intellectual donations, information provided by our

---

55   Quoted by John Pilger in a speech outside the Old Bailey, September 7, 2020.

sources. If the public believes in a three-month period that we should not be supported, that is the end of WikiLeaks. And that is unlike any democratically elected government."[56]

THE IDEAL MAN

"What is a gentleman? . . . The importance of being honourable, and keeping your word, and acting like a gentleman. It's someone who has the courage of their convictions, who doesn't bow to pressure, who doesn't exploit people who are weaker than they are, who acts in an honourable way. . . . [This] describes an ideal I believe men should strive for."[57]

PRISTINE STEEL REPLACED BY SCRAP

"It is from the revelation of truth that all else follows. Our buildings can only be as tall as their bricks are strong. Our civilization is only as strong as its ideas are true. When our buildings are erected by the corrupt, when their cement is cut with dirt, when pristine steel is replaced by scrap—our buildings

---

56 "WikiSecrets," interview by Martin Smith, PBS *Frontline*, aired May 24, 2011, https://wikileaks.org/WikiSecrets-Julian-Assange-Full.html.

57 Decca Aitkenhead, "Julian Assange: The Fugitive," *Guardian*, December 7, 2012, https://www.theguardian.com/media/2012/dec/07/julian-assange-fugitive-interview.

are not safe to live in. And when our media is corrupt, when our academics are timid, when our history is filled with half-truths and lies—our civilization will never be just. It will never reach to the sky. Our societies are intellectual shanty towns. Our beliefs about the world and each other have been created by the same system that has lied us into repeated wars that have killed millions."[58]

FOUNDING FATHERS GOT IT RIGHT

"We know what would be much worse off: if the state had the right to shut everyone up in the world at a point of a gun if those people were saying something that the state did not like. That is the situation that mirrors that in the Soviet Union and instantly corrupts the state and the people, because in the end, it is only the people working with the press that holds powerful groups like states to account. That system of scrutiny of the state is so sacrosanct in preventing democracies going astray that it must be kept open, and people must be kept free to exchange knowledge with each other, and the press must not

---

58   Statement by Julian Assange after Six Months in Ecuadorian Embassy, December 20, 2012, https://wikileaks.org/Statement-by-Julian-Assange-after.html.

be censored. Now, that is a lesson that the founding fathers of the U.S. learned with regard to censorship that was applied to them by the British. That is a lesson that has been learned in a number of countries that have themselves gone through revolutions after periods of dictatorship or abuse."[59]

CHOLERA OR GONORRHEA: CHOOSING DONALD TRUMP OR HILLARY CLINTON

"Well, you're asking me, do I prefer cholera or gonorrhea? Personally, I would prefer neither. . . . We know how politics works in the United States. Whatever political party gets into government is going to merge with the bureaucracy pretty damn fast. It will be in a position where it has some levers in its hand. And so, as a result, corporate lobbyists will move in to help control those levers. So it doesn't make much difference in the end. What does make a difference is political accountability, a general deterrence set to stop political organizations behaving in a corrupt manner."[60]

---

59 "WikiSecrets" interview.

60 "Julian Assange: Choosing between Trump or Clinton is Like Picking between Cholera or Gonorrhea," Democracy Now interview Part 2, July 25, 2016, https://www.democracynow.org/2016/7/25/julian_assange_choosing_between_trump_or.

KEEPING THE NATIONAL SECURITY SECTOR IN CHECK

"We represent certain values about freedom of speech. We also represent a tendency to keep the national security sector, in every country but especially the United States, in check. And that sector is becoming such a bloated part of U.S. society that it is making it difficult for Obama and other parts of the White House to implement policy. And in order to keep it in check, there needs to be proper investigative journalism done on it. It needs to be held accountable to the people by the press, like every other organization must be held accountable."[61]

MAKING CONCESSIONS THE PEOPLE WANT

"There was a big [cable] we did for Yemen, which revealed that [President Ali Abdullah Saleh] had conspired with the United States to have the U.S. bomb Yemen and say that the Yemeni Air Force did it. So that was a big revelation that we released in December of last year. Although the President is still there, he has been handing out tremendous concessions as a result. That's been happening throughout the Arab world

---

61   "WikiSecrets" interview.

now. . . . So, although I think we will see a few more go down, in the end it actually doesn't really matter whether the leader is removed or not. What matters is that the power structure of the government changes. If you make the concessions that the people want, you're actually nearly all of the way when you want to be a just and responsible elite."[62]

CONCERNED ABOUT HUMAN BEINGS

"We do not have national security concerns. We have concerns about human beings."[63]

A GOOD PUBLISHING POLICY

"It is clear that information should be published if there is no harm in publishing it. It is clear that our harm-minimization process has, to date, been completely successful in its goals. Therefore, we are correct in sticking to our promise to publish everything that is of diplomatic, political, ethical, or historical

62   Hans Ulrich Obrist, "In Conversation with Julian Assange, Part I," Journal #25, e-flux, May 2011, https://www.e-flux.com/journal/25/67875/in-conversation-with-julian-assange-part-i/.

63   Carole Cadwalladr, "Julian Assange, Monk of the Online Age who Thrives on Intellectual Battle," Guardian, August 1, 2010, https://www.theguardian.com/media/2010/aug/01/julian-assange-wikileaks-afghanistan.

significance, that has not been published before, and is being suppressed. It is a good policy. It works."[64]

HOLDING THE NATIONAL SECURITY SECTOR TO ACCOUNT

"One man's collaboration is another man's conspiracy. So any collaboration between a journalist and a source, between one media organization and another media organization, can be viewed, the Attorney General Justice [sic] [Eric] Holder says, as a conspiracy that flows through. That's a very danger-ous interpretation, and that interpretation must be resisted. And the *New York Times* must stand up, and it must hold the line that the traditional form of journalism that people have been doing in the United States, Sy [Seymour] Hersh and others, concerning the national security sector, calling up sources, saying, 'What do you know about this helicopter accident? What do you know about these abuse allegations that we've been hearing, and can you prove it?'—that needs to be protected at all costs, because if it is not protected, it will be the end of holding the national security sector to account.

---

64   Hans Ulrich Obrist, "In Conversation with Julian Assange, Part
II," Journal #26, e-flux, June 2011, https://www.e-flux.com/
journal/26/67921/in-conversation-with-julian-assange-part-ii/.

And the reality is that that sector makes up, directly and indirectly, some 30 to 40 percent of the entire U.S. economy. It is extremely powerful."[65]

---

65 "WikiSecrets" interview.

ACTIVISM

"People often ask, 'What can I do?' The answer is not so difficult. Learn how the world works. Challenge the statements, actions, and intentions of those who seek to control us behind the facades of democracy and monarchy. Unite in common purpose and common principle to design, build, document, finance, and defend. Learn. Challenge. Act. Now."[66]

FREE PRESS ACTIVISTS

"We are free press activists. It's not about saving the whales. It's about giving people the information they need to support whaling or not support whaling. Why? That is the raw ingredient that is needed to make a just and civil society and without that we're just sailing in the dark."[67]

---

66   Statement by Julian Assange after Six Months in Ecuadorian Embassy, December 20, 2012.

67   *60 Minutes Rewind*, interview by Steve Croft, January 30, 2011, https://www.youtube.com/watch?v=Ubknv_CxSUY.

CHANGING BEHAVIOR WITH SMALL AMOUNT OF INFORMATION

"In considering how unjust acts are caused, and what tends to promote them, and what promotes just acts, I saw that human beings are basically invariant. That is, their inclinations and biological temperament haven't changed much over thousands of years. Therefore the only playing field left is: what do they have and what do they know? What they have—that is, what resources they have at their disposal, how much energy they can harness, what food supplies they have and so on—is something that is fairly hard to influence. But what they know can be affected in a nonlinear way because when one person conveys information to another, they can convey it on to another, and another. . . . Therefore, you can change the behavior of many people with a small amount of information. The question then arises as to what kinds of information will produce behavior which is just and disincentivize behavior which is unjust?"[68]

---

68   Julian Assange, *When Google Met WikiLeaks*, OR Books, 2014, p. 67.

COURAGE IS CONTAGIOUS

"This is why Tiananmen Square is so heavily policed in China, because it's a congregation point where courage can spread like a contagion."[69]

QUALITY OF DISCOURSE IS LIMIT OF CIVILIZATION

"We have to educate each other. We have to celebrate those who reveal the truth and denounce those who poison our ability to comprehend the world that we live in. The quality of our discourse is the limit of our civilization."[70]

SECURE COMMUNICATIONS DURING REVOLUTIONARY PERIODS

"During revolutionary periods the people involved in the revolution need to be able to communicate in order to plan quickly, and they need to be able to pass around information about what is happening in their environment so that they can dynamically adapt to it and produce the next strategy. If

---

69 "In Conversation with Julian Assange, Part II," Hans Ulrich Obrist, Journal #26, e-flux, June 2011, https://www.e-flux.com/journal/26/67921/in-conversation-with-julian-assange-part-ii/.

70 Statement by Julian Assange after Six Months in Ecuadorian Embassy, December 20, 2012.

only the security services are able to communicate, and the government turns the mobile phone system off, the security services have a tremendous advantage. If you have a system where individuals are able to communicate securely and robustly despite what the security services are doing, then the security services will have to give more ground. It's not that the government is necessarily going to be overthrown, but rather they have to make more concessions."[71]

TRUE DEMOCRACY THE SUM OF RESISTANCE

"True democracy is not the White House. True democracy is not Canberra. True democracy is the resistance of people, armed with the truth, against lies, from Tahrir to right here in London. Every day, ordinary people teach us that democracy is free speech and dissent. For once we, the people, stop speaking out and stop dissenting, once we are distracted or pacified, once we turn away from each other, we are no longer free. For true democracy is the sum—is the sum—of our resistance."[72]

---

71   Assange, *When Google Met WikiLeaks,* p. 110.

72   Statement by Julian Assange after Six Months in Ecuadorian Embassy, December 20, 2012.

PROTECTING HUMAN RIGHTS DEFENDERS

"I am an activist, journalist, software programmer expert in cryptography, specialized in systems designed to protect human rights defenders."[73]

MOVING INFORMATION TO WHERE IT'S NEEDED

"In our work with Nawaat.org, who created Tunileaks, pushing the State Department cables past the regime's censorship into pre-revolutionary Tunisia, we saw first-hand the terrific power of the network for moving information to where it is needed, and it was tremendously rewarding to have been in a position, because of our efforts, to contribute to what was starting to happen there. I do not perceive that struggle for self-determination as distinct from our own."[74]

73   "Julian Assange, Man of the Year for Le Monde," *Le Monde*, December 24, 2010, https://www.lemonde.fr/documents-wikileaks/article/2010/12/24/julian-assange-homme-de-l-annee-pour-le-monde_1456426_1446239.html.

74   Julian Assange, with Jacob Appelbaum, Andy Müller-Maguhn, and Jérémie Zimmermann, *Cypherpunks: Freedom and the Future of the Internet*, OR Books, 2012, p. 158.

EITHER A PARTICIPANT IN HISTORY OR A VICTIM OF IT

"I think first it's necessary to have an understanding that one is either a participant in history or a victim of it, and that there is no other option. It is actually not possible to remove oneself from history, because of the nature of economic . . . and intellectual interaction. Hence, it is not possible to break oneself off. . . . Because no one wants to be a victim, one must therefore be a participant, and in being a participant, the most important thing to understand is that your behavior affects other people's behavior, and your courage will inspire actions. On the other hand, a lack of courage will suppress them."[75]

USING INFORMATION TO MAKE THE WORLD MORE JUST

"There's a universe of information, and we can imagine a sort of Platonic ideal in which we have an infinite horizon of information. It's similar to the concept of the Tower of Babel. Imagine a field before us composed of all the information that exists in the world—inside government computers, people's letters, things that have already been published, the stream

---

75   Obrist, "In Conversation with Julian Assange, Part II."

of information coming out of televisions, this total knowledge of all the world, both accessible and inaccessible to the public. We can as a thought experiment observe this field and ask: If we want to use information to produce actions that affect the world to make it more just, which information will do that? So what we ask for is a way to color the field of information before us, to take a yellow highlighter and mark the interesting bits—all the information that is most likely to have that effect on the world, which leads it toward the state we desire."[76]

EVERYONE ELSE MUST TAKE MY PLACE

"I am unbroken, albeit literally surrounded by murderers, but the days when I could read and speak and organize to defend myself, my ideals, and my people are over until I am free! Everyone else must take my place."[77]

---

76 "In Conversation with Julian Assange, Part I," Hans Ulrich Obrist, Journal #25, e-flux, May 2011, https://www.e-flux.com/journal/25/67875/in-conversation-with-julian-assange-part-i/.

77 Julian Assange, letter from Belmarsh Prison, published in *The Canary,* May 13, 2019, https://defend.wikileaks.org/2019/05/26/julian-assange-writes-a-letter-from-belmarsh-prison/.

RADICALIZATION OF INTERNET-EDUCATED YOUTH

"That's the most optimistic thing that is happening—the radicalization of internet-educated youth. People who are receiving their values from the internet and then, as they find them to be compatible, echoing them back. The echo back is now so strong that it drowns the original statements completely. The people that I've dealt with from the 1960s' radicals who helped liberate Greece and fight Salazar in Portugal, they say that this moment in time is the most similar there has been to what happened in that period of liberation movements. . . . The political education of apolitical technical people is extraordinary. Young people are going from apolitical to political. It is a very very interesting transition to see."[78]

COURAGE THE INTELLECTUAL MASTERY OF FEAR

"People often say, 'You are tremendously courageous in doing what you're doing.' And I say, 'No, you misunderstand what courage is. Courage is not the absence of fear. Only fools have no fear. Rather, courage is the intellectual mastery of fear by

---

78   Assange, *When Google Met WikiLeaks,* pp. 115–116.

understanding the true risks and opportunities of the situation and keeping those things in balance.'"[79]

FINDING EACH OTHER

"It is the nature of human beings that they lie and cheat and deceive. Organized groups of people who do not lie and cheat and deceive find each other and get together. Because they have that temperament, they are more efficient, because they are not lying and cheating and deceiving each other."[80]

TRUTH TOPPLED BEN ALI

"The population starts to know [because of the dissemination of the Tunisian cables], and they start to know in a way that's undeniable. And they also start to know that the United States knows, and the United States can't deny what was going on inside Tunisia. And then the elites within the country and without the country also know what is going on and know they can't deny it. So, a situation developed where it was not possible for the United States to support the Ben Ali regime and intervene in a revolution in Tunisia in the way that it might have. Similarly, it

79   Ibid., p. 138.

80   Ibid., p. 190.

was not possible for France to support Ben Ali or other partners in the same way that they might have been able to."[81]

TECHNOLOGY PERMITS THE SUBCULTURE

"You can argue this on both sides [whether the subculture creates the demand that leads to the creation of the technology, or whether the technology creates the subculture], but I think the technology permits the subculture. Once you have a whole bunch of young people who can communicate their ideas and values freely, then culture arises naturally. That culture comes out of experiences and harmonizing with other cultures and stuff already in the record, but it also just comes out of the temperament of young people—the desire to find allies and friends and share in a process and to remove power from old people!"[82]

POWER OF RESISTING TOGETHER

"The power of people speaking up and resisting together terrifies corrupt and undemocratic power. So much so that ordinary people here in the West are now the enemy of governments,

---

81   Democracy Now at the Frontline Club, https://www.democracynow. org/2012/8/16/from_our_archives_full_video_of_wikileaks_julian_ assange_philoso-pher_slavoj_iek_with_amy_goodman.

82   Assange, *When Google Met WikiLeaks*, p. 182.

an enemy to be watched, an enemy to be controlled and to be impoverished."[83]

PROCESS PART OF THE END GAME

"I think we can make some significant advances and perhaps it is the making of these advances and being involved in that struggle that is good for people. The process is part of the end game. It's not just to get somewhere in the end; rather this process of people feeling that it is worthwhile to be involved in that sort of struggle, is in fact worthwhile for people."[84]

THE WORLD WAS WATCHING

"Inside the embassy, after dark, I could hear teams of police swarming up into the building through the internal fire escape. But I knew there would be witnesses. And that is because of you. If the U.K. did not throw away the Vienna Conventions the other night, it is because the world was watching. And the world was watching because you were watching. The next time somebody tells you that it is pointless to defend the rights we

---

83   Statement by Julian Assange after Six Months in Ecuadorian Embassy, December 20, 2012.

84   Assange, *When Google Met WikiLeaks*, p. 190.

hold dear, remind them of your vigil in the dark outside the Embassy of Ecuador, and how, in the morning, the sun came up on a different world, and a courageous Latin American nation took a stand for justice."[85]

POWER OF THE PUBLIC SQUARE

"Most revolutions kick off in a crowd situation . . . all the time the regime is saying, 'This voice is an outcast voice. This is a minority. This is not popular opinion.' And what the media does is censor those voices and prevent people from understanding that actually what the state is saying is in the minority. And once people realize that their view is in the majority, then they understand that they physically have the numbers. And there's no better way to do that than in some kind of public square, which is why Tahrir Square in Egypt was so important, because everyone could see that they had the numbers."[86]

---

85   Official Statement by Julian Assange from the Ecuadorian Embassy, August 19, 2012, https://wikileaks.org/Official-Statement-by-Julian.html.

86   Democracy Now at the Frontline Club.

RUNNING AWAY TO FIGHT ANOTHER DAY

"I believe the most effective activists are those that fight and run away to fight another day, not those who fight and martyr themselves. That's about judgment—when to engage in the fight and when to withdraw so as to preserve your resources for the next fight."[87]

NEED FOR UNITY

"There is unity in the oppression. There must be absolute unity and determination in the response."[88]

A THOUSAND MORE CHELSEA MANNINGS

" . . . Manning's treatment has been intended to send a signal to people of conscience in the U.S. government who might seek to bring wrongdoing to light. This strategy has spectacularly backfired, as recent months have proven. Instead, the Obama administration is demonstrating that there is no place in its

---

87 Assange, *When Google Met WikiLeaks,* p. 137.

88 Official Statement by Julian Assange from the Ecuadorian Embassy, August 19, 2012.

system for people of conscience and principle. As a result, there will be a thousand more [Chelsea] Mannings."[89]

LEARNING FROM LOOKING BACK

"You should always look back in the past and think 'I would do something differently,' because otherwise you haven't learned."[90]

AN ABSOLUTE HERO: THE SOURCE(S) FOR THE COLLATERAL MURDER VIDEO

"Our source or sources for this dramatic military material and the State Department material that we have been releasing over the past seven months is the greatest whistleblower that has ever existed, is the bravest source that we know about in journalism. And to that extent, [the source is] an absolute hero. [The source] has been a catalyst for the revolutions that are happening in the Middle East, something that we thought was never possible; has

---

89   Statement by Julian Assange on Today's Sentencing of [Chelsea] Manning, August 21, 2013, https://wikileaks.org/Statement-by-Julian-Assange-on,267.html. On January 16, 2017, President Obama granted Chelsea Manning clemency and commuted the remaining eighteen years of her thirty-five-year sentence to four months.

90   "WikiSecrets," interview by Martin Smith, PBS Frontline, documentary aired May 24, 2011, https://wikileaks.org/WikiSecrets-JulianAssange-Full.html.

been a catalyst for important political change happening in Peru and other parts of South America; for exposing corruption in the Indian Parliament, which has walked out over four times as a result of material in the State Department cables. That individual or individuals operating as a switch to enable a certain course of action has done more for the world in the past, done more for the world than any other person that I can think of."[91]

TRUTH IS THE ONLY WAY

"You have to start with the truth. The truth is the only way that we can get anywhere. Because any decision-making that is based upon lies or ignorance can't lead to a good conclusion."[92]

A DARING ADVENTURE

"If we can only live once, then let it be a daring adventure that draws on all our powers. Let it be with similar types whose hearts and heads we may be proud of. Let our grandchildren

---

91   Ibid. In his unwavering promise to never reveal a source, Julian did not reveal Chelsea Manning as having been the source of the Collateral Murder video as well as hundreds of thousands of other leaks that formed the basis of the Iraq and Afghanistan war logs.

92   Carole Cadwalladr, "Julian Assange, Monk of the Online Age who Thrives on Intellectual Battle," *The Guardian*, August 1, 2010, https://www.theguardian.com/media/2010/aug/01/julian-assange-wikileaks-afghanistan.

delight to find the start of our stories in their ears but the endings all around in their wandering eyes. The whole universe or the structure that perceives it is a worthy opponent, but try as I may, I cannot escape the sound of suffering. Perhaps as an old man I will take great comfort in pottering around in a lab and gently talking to students in the summer evening and will accept suffering with insouciance. But not now; men in their prime, if they have convictions are tasked to act on them."[93]

INSPIRING A COURSE OF ENNOBLING ACTION

"To radically shift regime behavior we must think clearly and boldly, for if we have learned anything, it is that regimes do not want to be changed. We must think beyond those who have gone before us, and discover technological changes that embolden us with ways to act in which our forebears could not. Firstly, we must understand what aspect of government or neocorporatist behavior we wish to change or remove. Secondly, we must develop a way of thinking about this behavior that is strong enough to carry us through the mire of politically

---

93   Julian Assange, "Witnessing," January 3, 2007, from "Selected Correspondence," http://web.archive.org/web/20071020051936/http://iq.org/#Witnessing.

distorted language, and into a position of clarity. Finally, we must use these insights to inspire within us and others a course of ennobling, and effective action."[94]

94   Julian Assange, "State and Terrorist Conspiracies," blog of November
      10, 2006, http://cryptome.org/0002/ja-conspiracies.pdf.

CENSORSHIP

[Censorship] is always an opportunity, because it reveals a fear of reform. And if an organization is expressing a fear of reform, it is also expressing the fact that it can be reformed.[95]

AI FOR DISCOURSE CONTROL

"While the internet has brought about a revolution in people's ability to educate themselves and others, the resulting democratic phenomenon has shaken existing establishments to their core. Google, Facebook, and their Chinese equivalents, which are socially, logistically, and financially integrated with existing elites, have moved to re-establish discourse control. This is not simply a corrective action. Undetectable mass social influence powered by artificial intelligence is an existential threat to humanity. While still in its infancy the trends are clear and of a geometric nature. The phenomenon differs from traditional attempts to shape

---

95   "In Conversation with Julian Assange, Part I," Hans Ulrich Obrist, Journal #25, e-flux, May 2011, https://www.e-flux.com/journal/25/67875/in-conversation-with-julian-assange-part-i/.

cultural and political phenomena by operating at a scale, speed, and increasingly at a subtlety that eclipses human capacities."[96]

CRYPTOGRAPHY OR SELF-CENSORSHIP

"People will have to think about it [cryptography]. . . . They will either think, 'I need to be careful about what I say, I need to conform,' the whole time, in every interaction. Or they will think, 'I need to master little components of this technology and install things that protect me so I'm able to express my thoughts freely and communicate freely with my friends and people I care about.' If people don't take that second step then we'll have a universal political correctness, because even when people are communicating with their closest friends they will be self-censors and will remove themselves as political actors from the world."[97]

RATTLING THE CAGE

"We should always see censorship, actually, as a very positive sign, and the attempts toward censorship as a sign that

---

96   Statement to the "Organizing Resistance to Internet Censorship" webinar organized by the World Socialist Website, January 16, 2018, https://www.wsws.org/en/articles/2018/01/18/assa-j18.html.

97   Julian Assange, with Jacob Appelbaum, Andy Müller-Maguhn, and Jérémie Zimmermann, *Cypherpunks: Freedom and the Future of the Internet*, OR Books, 2012, pp. 64–65.

the society is not yet completely sewn up, not yet completely fiscalized, but still has some political dimension to it—i.e. that what people believe, think, and feel, and the words that they listen to actually matter. . . . We managed to speak and give information at such volume and of such intensity that people actually were forced to respond. It is rare that they are forced to respond. So, I think this is one of the first positive symptoms I've seen from the United States in a while, that actually if you speak at this level, the cage can be rattled a bit, and people can be forced to respond."[98]

INTELLECTUAL RECORD DISAPPEARING

"Parts of our intellectual record are disappearing in such a way that we cannot even tell that they have ever existed."[99]

THE CENSORSHIP PYRAMID

"You can think about censorship as a pyramid. This pyramid only has its tip sticking out of the sand, and that is by intention. The tip is public—libel suits, murders of journalists, cameras

---

98   Democracy Now at the Frontline Club, https://www.democracynow.
      org/2012/8/16/from_our_archives_full_video_of_wikileaks_julian_
      assange_philoso-pher_slavoj_iek_with_amy_goodman.

99   Obrist, "In Conversation with Julian Assange, Part I."

being snatched by the military, and so on—publicly declared censorship. But that is the smallest component. Under the tip, the next layer is all those people who don't want to be at the tip, who engage in self-censorship to not end up there. Then the next layer is all the forms of economic inducement or patronage inducement that are given to people to write about one thing or another. The next layer down is raw economy—what it is economic to write about, even if you don't include the economic factors from higher up the pyramid. Then the next layer is the prejudice of readers who only have a certain level of education, so therefore on one hand they are easy to manipulate with false information, and on the other hand you can't even tell them something sophisticated that is true. The last layer is distribution—for example, some people just don't have access to information in a particular language. So that is the censorship pyramid."[100]

CENSORSHIP CAUSE FOR CELEBRATION

"I often say that censorship is always cause for celebration. It is always an opportunity because it reveals fear of reform. It

---

100 Assange, *Cypherpunks,* pp. 123–124.

means that the power position is so weak that you have got to care what people think."[101]

EXTRAJUDICIAL STATE CENSORSHIP WORKING THROUGH THE PRIVATE SECTOR

"I think the attacks on us by Visa, PayPal, Mastercard, Bank of America, PostFinance, Moneybookers, and other U.S. companies—predominantly banks and financial intermediaries—is the most interesting revelation that has come out of what we've been doing. Like the Pentagon Papers case, the reaction and overreaction of the state and other groups involved in it will be seen to be one of the most important outcomes of the revelation itself. What we see is that the United States, in its reaction to us, behaved no differently than the Soviet Union in the 1960s towards Solzhenitsyn, and in the 1970s towards Sakharov, just in a more modern way. Previous censorship actions in the West have been more subtle, more nuanced, and harder to see, but here we have a case of absolutely naked, flagrant, extrajudicial state censorship working through the private sector."[102]

---

101 Julian Assange, *When Google Met WikiLeaks*, OR Books, 2014, p. 121.

102 "In Conversation with Julian Assange, Part II," Hans Ulrich Obrist, Journal #26, e-flux, June 2011, https://www.e-flux.com/journal/26/67921/in-conversation-with-julian-assange-part-ii/. Ten days after the

ERASURE OF HISTORY

"History is not only modified, it has ceased to have ever existed. . . . It is the undetectable erasure of history in the West, and that's just post-publication censorship. Pre-publication self-censorship is much more extreme but often hard to detect. We've seen that with Cablegate as WikiLeaks works with different media partners all over the world, so we can see which ones censor our material. . . . There are lots of examples."[103]

ACADEMIC FRAUD

"This closing of ranks within the scholar class around the interests of the Pentagon and the State Department is, in itself, worthy of analysis. The censorship of cables from international relations journals is a type of academic fraud. To quietly exclude primary

---

launch of Cablegate, which was followed by an avalanche of lethal threats and aggressive retaliation, an illegal financial blockade was imposed on WikiLeaks by Bank of America, Visa, Mastercard, PayPal, and Western Union. The attack destroyed 95 percent of its revenue (see also fn. 161), and led the organization at the time to rely primarily upon cryptocurrency companies for financial transfers (https://wikileaks.org/Banking-Blockade.html). Commented Julian, "Those discouraging financial attacks will be encouraging to other organizations in the sense that we got through them. Regardless of whether we win or lose, they provide encouragement for people to set up alternative financial conveyance structures, and that is a really positive outcome" (Obrist op. cit.).

103   Assange, *Cypherpunks,* pp. 121–122.

sources for non-academic reasons is to lie by omission. But it points to a larger insight: the distortion of the field of international relations and related disciplines by the proximity of its academic structures to the U.S. government. Its structures do not even have the independence of the frequently deferent *New York Times*, which, while it engaged in various forms of cable censorship, at least managed to publish over a hundred."[104]

INTELLIGENCE AND INTELLIGENCE AGENCIES

"As opposed to what is sometimes put about, WikiLeaks is not an organization that hates intelligence agencies—far from it. At its very base, the idea of intelligence is an optimistic one—it is that one can understand the world, one can apply intelligence to understand. The problem is the corruption of those agencies and that corruption comes about because of secrecy."[105]

WHO CONTROLS THE PRESENT CONTROLS THE PAST

"Important bits of recent history that were relevant to an ongoing presidential campaign in the United States were pulled out

104 WikiLeaks, with introduction by Julian Assange, *The WikiLeaks Files: The World According to U.S. Empire*, Verso, 2015, p. 11.

105 Julian Assange, Talk at Oxford Union Society, via video link, January 23, 2013, https://www.youtube.com/watch?v=4vQNWYnQjUE.

of the intellectual record. . . . Not only have they ceased to exist, they have ceased to have ever existed. It is the modern implementation of Orwell's dictum: 'Who controls the past controls the future; who controls the present controls the past'—because all records of the past are stored physically in the present."[106]

USE OF COPYRIGHT TO SUPPRESS REVELATIONS

"WikiLeaks, in practice, receives many copyright threats. According to the more strict definitions of copyright, every single thing we publish breaches copyright. In the more grounded interpretations of copyright, such as those that exist in the United States Constitution, nothing we publish is a breach of copyright because copyright was originally designed—at least following its original political argument and justification—to potentiate a greater economy. It was not there to protect the internal documents of a company from being exposed to the public. And it certainly was not there to protect government documents in cases where the Crown claims copyright over all government documents. The use of copyright to suppress revelations of the abuse of power by companies or governments is, in itself, an abuse of these basic notions that authors, rather

---

106 Assange, *When Google Met WikiLeaks,* p. 83.

than opportunists, should be making the majority of money from the production of books, and those basic notions are what led to the development of copyrights in the first place."[107]

AN ENCROACHING, PRIVATIZED CENSORSHIP REGIME

"In the U.K. right now, there are three hundred secret gag orders. Those are gag orders that not only prevent the press from reporting corruption and abuse; they prevent the press from reporting that the press has been gagged. This is not the liberal democracy that we had all dreamed of. This is an encroaching, privatized censorship regime. And just like everything else in the West that becomes privatized and fiscalized, censorship also is not only a mechanism that is applied by the state: it is something that can be hijacked by wealthy plutocrats, by big companies, to use the coercive mechanisms of the state through the judicial system, through unequal access to the judicial system, through patronage networks, to have material removed permanently from the historical record."[108]

---

107 Obrist, "In Conversation with Julian Assange, Part II."

108 Speech at Oslo Freedom Forum, April 26, 2010, https://www.religiousforums.com/threads/transcript-of-julian-assange-wikileaks-speech-2010-oslo-freedom-forum-april-2010.101236/.

REVEALS WEAKNESS, NOT STRENGTH

"When organizations or governments of various kinds attempt to contain knowledge and suppress it, they are giving you the most important information you need to know: that there is something worth looking at to see if it should be exposed and that censorship expresses weakness, not strength."[109]

DISAPPEARING THE PAST WITH DIGITAL ARCHIVES

"With digital archives, with these digital repositories of our intellectual record, control over the present allows one to perform an absolutely untraceable removal of the past. More than ever before, the past can be made to completely, utterly, and irrevocably disappear in an undetectable way."[110]

TRUTH IS ALL WE HAVE

"The U.S. government, or rather, those regrettable elements in it that hate truth, liberty, and justice, want to cheat their way into my extradition and death, rather than letting the

---

109   Obrist, "In Conversation with Julian Assange, Part I."
110   Ibid.

public hear the truth, for which I have won the highest awards in journalism and have been nominated seven times for the Nobel Peace Prize. Truth, ultimately, is all we have."[111]

111 Assange, letter from Belmarsh Prison, published in *The Canary*, May 13, 2019, https://defend.wikileaks.org/2019/05/26/julian-assange-writes-a-letter-from-belmarsh-prison/.

EMPIRE

Our beliefs about the world and each other have been created by the same system that has lied us into repeated wars that have killed millions.[112]

EXTRA-TERRITORIAL LAND GRAB

"To look at this from a geopolitical perspective, what is happening is not simply an increasing tendency towards authoritarianism in the West. There is a desire, and a method being erected, for the United States principally, to engage in an extra-territorial land-grab through the abuse of law. It is attempting to apply its jurisdiction to all countries in the world, to reach into other countries and destroy their sovereignty by demanding that its laws apply to their territory. Now, if you control the laws of a foreign country, if you say that your laws apply to the interior of a foreign country, this is the same as having effective

---

112 Statement by Julian Assange after Six Months in Ecuadorian Embassy, December 20, 2012.

control over the population of a foreign country—which is the same as, in a way, annexing that foreign country. The United States has been doing this in a unilateral manner, where it claims universal jurisdiction in relation to everything that it says has to do with national security, including publishing."[113]

UNDERSTANDING THE WORLD'S SOLE REMAINING EMPIRE

"Cultures and economies communicate using all manner of techniques across the regions and years of their existence, from the evolution of jokes shared virally between friends to the diffusion of prices across trade routes. This does not by itself make an empire. The structured attempt at managing an extended cultural and economic system using communications is the hallmark of empire. And it is the records of these communications, never intended to be dissected, and so especially vulnerable to dissection, that form the basis for understanding the nature of the world's sole remaining 'empire.'"[114]

---

113 Address to the UN Human Rights Council (from the Ecuadorian Embassy), May 26, 2015, excerpt "The U.S. Is Applying Its Jurisdiction to Other Countries," on TheWikiLeaksChannel, June 7, 2019, https://www.youtube.com/watch?v=0c4lD6rdgks.

114 WikiLeaks, with introduction by Julian Assange, *The WikiLeaks Files: The World According to U.S. Empire*, Verso, 2015, p. 3.

HOW TO FIX THINGS

"The only way to fix things is this: Change the policies. Stop spying on the world. Eradicate secret law. Cease indefinite detention without trial. Stop assassinating people. Stop invading other countries and sending young Americans off to kill and be killed. Stop the occupations and discontinue the secret wars. Stop eating the young: Edward Snowden, Barrett Brown, Jeremy Hammond, Aaron Swartz, Gottfrid Svartholm, Jacob Appelbaum, and [Chelsea] Manning."[115]

THREATENED BY A WILD COLONIAL BOY

"They must feel that they are weak. How could this very establishment in the United Kingdom, which has been in power for hundreds of years, feel threatened? It's quite sophisticated after all. It has many different components: the intelligence services, the banks, the landed gentry, the oligarchs from Russia who have come here and invested, the commercial media, it has the BBC which is the big propaganda organism that helps keep the country cohesive. It is quite a sophisticated power structure

---

115 Statement by Julian Assange after One Year in Ecuadorian Embassy, June 22, 2013, https://wikileaks.org/Statement-by-Julian-Assange-after,249.html.

with these interplaying parts. How could they feel threatened by a wild colonial boy from Australia who has arrived from overseas?"[116]

"DON'T BE EVIL" EMPIRE STILL AN EMPIRE

"If the future of the internet is to be Google, that should be of serious concern to people all over the world . . . for whom the internet embodies the promise of an alternative to U.S. cultural, economic, and strategic hegemony. A 'don't be evil' empire is still an empire."[117]

COMMUNICATIONS MEDIUM IS THE EMPIRE

"The study of empires has long been the study of their communications. Carved into stone or inked into parchment, empires from Babylon to the Ming Dynasty left records of the organizational center communicating with its peripheries. However, by the 1950s students of historical empires realized that somehow the communications medium *was* the empire. Its methods for organizing the inscription,

---

116 Tariq Ali and Margaret Kunstler, eds., *In Defense of Julian Assange*, OR Books, 2019, pp. 176–177.

117 Julian Assange, *When Google Met WikiLeaks*, OR Books, 2014, pp. 47–48.

transportation, indexing, and storage of its communications, and for designating who was authorized to read and write them, in a real sense *constituted* the empire. When the methods an empire used to communicate changed, the empire also changed."[118]

TRUE COST OF EMPIRE

"Only by approaching this corpus [the U.S. State Department cables], holistically—over and above the documentation of each individual abuse, each localized atrocity—does the true human cost of empire heave into view."[119]

DIGITAL COLONIALISM PERPETRATED BY SILICON VALLEY

"The long-term effect is a tendency towards conformity, because controversy is eliminated. An American mindset is being fostered and spread to the rest of the world because they find this mindset to be uncontroversial among themselves. That is literally a type of digital colonialism; non-U.S. cultures are being colonized by a mindset of what is

---

118 WikiLeaks, *The WikiLeaks Files*, p. 2.

119 Ibid., p. 6.

tolerable to the staff and investors of a few Silicon Valley companies. The cultural standard of what is a taboo and what is not becomes a U.S. standard, where U.S. exceptionalism is uncontroversial."[120]

CONFLICT SITUATION WITH THE MOST POWERFUL EMPIRE

"They are talking about the Swedish case, we are talking about the Swedish case, and no one is now talking about the case that was there in the beginning and is still ongoing, which is, as far as I am concerned, a great danger to me and to the organization as a whole, which is this massive espionage investigation. Let's be serious: we are in a conflict situation with the largest, most powerful empire—that's what it is—that has ever existed. In such a situation, it's remarkable to survive at all."[121]

---

120 "We Are Drowning in Material," interview by Michael Sontheimer, *Spiegel International*, July 20, 2015, https://www.spiegel.de/ international/world/spiegel-interview-with-wikileaks-head-julian- assange-a-1044399.html.

121 Juan Pancorbo and Clara López Rubio, dirs., *Hacking Justice*, Mediasur-Inselfilm, 2017.

DISPARITY OF INFORMATION

"The response of the United States to the release of the WikiLeaks materials betrays a belief that its power resides in a disparity of information: ever more knowledge for the empire, ever less for its subjects."[122]

---

122 WikiLeaks, *The WikiLeaks Files*, p. 18.

INTERNET

In the undreamt of political education in human history, there has never been such a moment when so many people from so many places have seen what the world is really like, what their place in the world is, what the place and behavior of others near to them truly is.[123]

TAKING ON A GENERATION IS A LOSING BATTLE

"Edward Snowden is one of us. [Chelsea] Manning is one of us. They are young, technically minded people from the generation that Barack Obama betrayed. They are the generation that grew up on the internet, and were shaped by it. The U.S. government is always going to need intelligence analysts and systems administrators, and they are going to have to hire them from this generation and the ones that follow it. One day, their generation will run the NSA, the CIA, and the FBI. This

---

123 "The First Globally Recognized Value of the Internet is the Right to Communicate," TheWikiLeaksChannel, June 24, 2019, https://www.youtube.com/user/TheWikiLeaksChannel/videos.

isn't a phenomenon that is going away. This is inevitable. And by trying to crush these young whistleblowers with espionage charges, the U.S. government is taking on a generation, and that is a battle it is going to lose."[124]

OUR PLATONIC REALM

"The platonic nature of the internet, ideas and information flows, is debased by its physical origins. Its foundations are fiber optic cable lines stretching across the ocean floors, satellites spinning above our heads, computer servers housed in buildings in cities from New York to Nairobi. Like the soldier who slew Archimedes with a mere sword, so too could an armed militia take control of the peak development of Western civilization, our platonic realm."[125]

TRANSITIONING INTO A *DEMOS*

"Alongside the changes on the streets [in 2011 across Europe, Latin America, and elsewhere], the internet was rapidly

---

124 Statement by Julian Assange after One Year in Ecuadorian Embassy, June 22, 2013.

125 Julian Assange, with Jacob Appelbaum, Andy Müller-Maguhn, and Jérémie Zimmermann, *Cypherpunks: Freedom and the Future of the Internet*, OR Books, 2012, p. 3.

transitioning from an apathetic communications medium into a *demos—a people* with a shared culture, shared values, and shared aspirations. It had become a place where history happens, a place people identified with and even felt they *came from*."[126]

PRIMARY TOOL OF EMANCIPATION

"The internet has become this generation's primary tool of emancipation. There's a lot of effort being put into trying to stop the internet working in the way it was meant to work, which is as a universal communications medium with which we can all communicate with each other across the world, to share our knowledge of the world, and together deal with the most significant problems we have at an individual level, at a group level, and at international level. . . . What is fantastic and unavoidable is that the internet generation is developing its own culture, its own consensus, and its own political view, and it is so much better informed than anything that existed before. . . . Young people are vastly more worldly and sophisticated than even ten years ago as a result of the internet. Their views about what is wrong and what is right are being

126 Julian Assange, *When Google Met WikiLeaks*, OR Books, 2014, p. 10.

internationalized as a result of education about how we are all living our lives."[127]

TOP OF THE PYRAMID OF THE NEOLIBERAL SYSTEM

"The internet is underpinned by extremely complex trade interactions between optical fiber manufacturers, semi-conductor manufacturers, mining companies that dig all this stuff up, and all the financial lubricants to make the trade happen, courts to enforce private property laws and so on. So it really is the top of the pyramid of the whole neoliberal system."[128]

THE FIRST GLOBALLY RECOGNIZED RIGHT OF THE INTERNET

"In the undreamt of political education in human history, there has never been such a moment when so many people from so many places have seen what the world is really like, what their place in the world is, what the place and behavior of others near to them truly is. From that there has been a distillation of values . . . the distillation of the first value of our

---

127   Julian Assange, "Cyber Terrorism," excerpt from talk at Oxford Union Society, via video link, January 23, 2013, https://www.youtube.com/watch?v=WJCL9S3Rlfk.

128   Assange, *Cypherpunks*, p. 27.

new global civilization. And that first value is something that is coupled to the network itself: it is the right to communicate, the right to speak what we believe, the right to receive information from others. It is those rights which are associated with United Nations Article 19, the right to receive and impart information in any medium across frontiers."[129]

MOST IMPORTANT DEVICE FOR REVEALING TRUTH

"The internet has become the most important device for revealing the truth, at least since the beginning of the printing press. It has become the number one antidote to TV. Democracies are always lied into war. The Iraq War was the result of lies. The increased involvement of the United States in Vietnam was a result of the Gulf of Tonkin incident, another lie. It's not just lies by intelligence analysts, it's lies by the big media machine. And what is in the big media machine? Well, it's the various institutions that get too comfortable and too close to the table of power, the very table that they are meant to be reporting on and policing and getting into the historic record. Now, working against that trend and against that current of

---

129 "The First Globally Recognized Value of the Internet is the Right to Communicate."

corrupt, powerful organizations producing a distorted perspective of the world has been the internet. For the first time in history, that has allowed one person with some truth to speak to every single person who wants to hear that truth."[130]

RAPIDITY OF MASS CONSENSUS

"Despite this mass surveillance, mass communication has led to millions of people being able to come to a fast consensus. If you can go from a normal position to a new mass consensus position very quickly, then while the state might be able to see it developing, there's not enough time to formulate an effective response."[131]

TRAVELING OUT TO THE WORLD

"Australia's very isolated. If you're a curious person, you want to travel elsewhere. But if you're a teenager you can't afford to travel. Air flights were expensive. I certainly couldn't afford it; I didn't even have a passport. But using your mind you could

---

130 "Fighting Propaganda," TheWikiLeaksChannel, May 15, 2019, https://www.youtube.com/watch?v=Ffgi9z7v0aU.

131 Assange, *Cypherpunks*, p. 23.

travel out. So I traveled out on this new network and started understanding its power structures."[132]

INDEXING SYSTEM FOR THE TOWER OF BABEL

"All creative works that can be put into digital form can be linked in a way that depends on nothing but the intellectual content of the material itself. . . . And so, if we have a blog post, it will have a unique name. And if the post changes, the name will change, but the post and the name are always completely coupled. If we have a sonata and a recording of it, then it has a unique name. If we have a film in digitized form, then it has a unique name. If we have a leaked, classified document that we release, it has a unique name. And it's not possible to change the underlying document without changing the name. I think it's very important—a kind of indexing system for the Tower of Babel, or pure knowledge."[133]

---

132 Tariq Ali and Margaret Kunstler, eds., *In Defense of Julian Assange*, OR Books, 2019, pp. 173–174.

133 "In Conversation with Julian Assange, Part I," Hans Ulrich Obrist, Journal #25, e-flux, May 2011, https://www.e-flux.com/journal/25/67875/in-conversation-with-julian-assange-part-i/.

GREATEST THEFT OF WEALTH

"The merger of our societies with the internet, and the internet with our societies, has allowed a really amazing lateral transfer of information where we're able to learn from each other much more than we could. On the other hand, it has allowed state intelligence organizations and the contractors who work for them to collect more information. It is in some ways the greatest theft of wealth that has ever occurred."[134]

POLITICAL SANCTION CATCHING UP TO FAST WEALTH MOVEMENT

"The big issue with globalization is that you can be an asshole and move your money elsewhere. Fast EFTs, fast wealth movements, fast signing of contracts (which are a type of wealth movement)—these encourage opportunism. Because money can move faster than political sanction, you can just keep moving the money through the system, and growing it as it moves through the system, and having it become more and more powerful, and by the time the moral outrage comes to stop it, it's too late, it has gone. So what's happening now on the

---

134 Juan Pancorbo and Clara López Rubio, dirs., *Hacking Justice*, Mediasur-Inselfilm, 2017.

internet is that political sanction . . . is now able to move a lot faster than it did before—possibly as fast as money."[135]

PRIVATIZATION OF WORDS

"The problem with URLs is that they are authority names. A URL goes to some company or organization, and the name is completely controlled by the company or organization, which means that Project Gutenberg could conceivably copy the Talmud over the *King James Bible* but the 'URL name' would remain the same. It is simply up to the whim of whoever controls that domain name. . . . We all now suffer from the privatization of words, a privatization of those fundamental abstractions human beings use to communicate. The way we refer to our common intellectual record is becoming privatized, with different parts of it being soaked up into domain names controlled by private companies, institutions, or states."[136]

PUBLISHING PURELY FOR ALTRUISTIC REASONS

"It's a classic best-use case for the internet: cheap publication means that we can have many more types of publishers,

---

135 Assange, *When Google Met WikiLeaks*, p. 184.

136 Obrist, "In Conversation with Julian Assange, Part I."

including self-subsidizing publishers. People are able to publish purely for ideological reasons or for altruistic reasons, because the costs of altruism in relation to publishing are not so high that you can't do it."[137]

PROTECTING THE HISTORICAL RECORD

"So, that quest to protect the historical record and enable everyone to be a contributor to the historical record is something that I have been involved in for about twenty years, in one way or another. So that means protecting people who contribute to our shared intellectual record, and it also means protecting publishers and encouraging distribution of the historical record to everyone who needs to know about it. After all, an historical record that has something interesting in it that you can't find is no record at all."[138]

A NEW PRE-REVOLUTIONARY MOMENT

"This is a new pre-revolutionary moment, just like when you had industrialization and as a result you developed skilled

---

137 Assange, *When Google Met WikiLeaks*, p. 85.

138 Democracy Now at the Frontline Club, August 16, 2012, https://www. democracynow.org/2012/8/16/from_our_archives_full_video_of_ wikileaks_julian_assange_philoso-pher_slavoj_iek_with_amy_goodman.

workers, and once skilled workers developed the political consciousness as to their own power and position in society, they could act to change the society. The internet generation is in exactly that same position—perhaps in an even more advantageous position because the internet is also involved not merely in the control structure of these great and powerful institutions but it is involved intimately in spreading our culture, spreading our knowledge about the world. It is a replacement media, and it is unignorable."[139]

139 Assange, "Cyber Terrorism."

JOURNALISM

We've actually played inside the rules—we didn't go out to get the material. We operated just like any U.S. publisher operates.[140]

HISTORY OF JOURNALISM

"There's a question as to what sort of information is important in the world, what sort of information can achieve reform. And there's a lot of information. Information that organizations are spending economic effort into concealing, that's a really good signal that when the information gets out, there's a hope of it doing some good, because the organizations that know it best, that know it from the inside out, are spending work to conceal it. And that's what we've found in practice. And that's what the history of journalism is."[141]

---

140 *60 Minutes Rewind*, interview by Steve Croft, January 30, 2011, https://www.youtube.com/watch?v=Ubknv_CxSUY.

141 "Why the World Needs WikiLeaks," interview by Chris Anderson, TED, July 19, 2010, https://www.ted.com/talks/julian_assange_why_the_world_needs_wikileaks.

CHANGING PERCEPTION OF THOSE PAYING

"The people in Baghdad, the people in Iraq, the people in Afghanistan—they don't need to see the video [of collateral murders]. They see it every day. It's not going to change their opinion; it's not going to change their perception. . . . It will change the perception and opinion of the people who are paying for it all. And that's our hope."[142]

BLOGGERS SERVE THE FUNCTION OF THE PUBLIC SQUARE

"I've often lambasted bloggers as people who just want to demonstrate peer value conformity and who don't actually do any original news, don't do any original work. . . . Often we find that all these left-wing bloggers do not descend on a fresh cable from Panama, revealing, as it did today, that the United States has declared the right to board one-third of all ships in the world without any justification. . . . Rather, they read the front page of the *New York Times* and go, 'I disagree' or 'I agree.' . . . That hypocrisy of saying that you care about a situation, but not actually doing the work, is something that has angered me. But it does serve an important function. The function that it serves is

142 "Why the World Needs WikiLeaks," interview, TED, July 19, 2010.

the function of the square. It is to show the number of voices that are lining up, on one side or another."[143]

TREATING THE READER WITH RESPECT

"Newspapers don't have physical room for the primary source; now that there is physical room for the primary source we should create a standard that it should be there. People can deviate from this standard, but if they deviate from the standard and can't be bothered to provide us with the primary source data then why should we pay any attention to what they are writing? They are not treating the reader with respect."[144]

PENETRATION OF TRUTH INTO MAINSTREAM MEDIA A LASTING LEGACY

"An interesting phenomena has developed amongst the journalists who work in these very large organizations that are close to power and negotiate with power at the highest levels, which is the journalists, having read our material and having been forced to go

---

143 Democracy Now at the Frontline Club, August 16, 2012, https://www.democracynow.org/2012/8/16/from_our_archives_full_video_of_wikileaks_julian_assange_philoso-pher_slavoj_iek_with_amy_goodman.

144 Julian Assange, *When Google Met WikiLeaks*, OR Books, 2014, 127.

through it to pull out stories, have themselves become educated and radicalized. And that is an ideological penetration of the truth into all these mainstream media organizations. And that, to some degree, may be one of the lasting legacies over the past year."[145]

PACIFIED INTO BEING REACTIVE

"These groups [bloggers, Wikipedia-types, leftist intellectuals] don't know how to lead the intellectual debate. They've been pacified into being reactive by the presence of the mainstream press. . . . The aim of most non-professional writers is to take the cheapest possible content that permits them to demonstrate their value of conformity to the widest possible selection of the group that they wish to gain the favor of."[146]

SCIENTIFIC JOURNALISM

"I have been pushing this idea of scientific journalism—that things must be precisely cited with the original source, and as much of the information as possible should be put in the public domain so that people can look at it, just like in science so that

---

145 Democracy Now at the Frontline Club.

146 "In Conversation with Julian Assange, Part I," Hans Ulrich Obrist, Journal #25, e-flux, May 2011, https://www.e-flux.com/journal/25/67875/in-conversation-with-julian-assange-part-i/.

you can test to see whether the conclusion follows from the experimental data. Otherwise the journalist probably just made it up. In fact, that is what happens all the time: people just make it up. They make it up to such a degree that we are led to war."[147]

MESSENGERS FOR THE STATE DEPARTMENT

"As the diplomatic apparatus of the United States, the State Department is directly involved in putting a friendly face on empire, concealing its underlying mechanics. Every year, more than $1 billion is budgeted for 'public diplomacy,' a circumlocutory term for outward-facing propaganda. Public diplomacy explicitly aims to influence journalists and civil society, so that they serve as conduits for State Department messaging."[148]

DELEGATING SOURCE MATERIAL TO OTHER JOURNALISTS

"We're a small organization. When we're in a position, say with Cablegate, where we have three thousand volumes of material that are very important to get out to the public in a responsible manner, that have the potential for great change—for example this recent

---

147 Assange, *When Google Met WikiLeaks,* p. 126.

148 WikiLeaks, with introduction by Julian Assange, *The WikiLeaks Files: The World According to U.S. Empire*, Verso, 2015, p. 5.

revolution in Tunisia—it is logistically impossible, so instead our organization delegates its excess source material to other journalists who will have more impact and who will do a better job."[149]

MOTIVATIONS OF AN EDITOR

"Would WikiLeaks turn down tens of thousands of documents from a political party in an election? I think the interesting question is: Would another media organization turn it down? These questions about the motivations of an editor or a proprietor, actually, I think they're fair, I think it is fair to ask those questions. I don't think the answers are very fair. But do you ever hear those questions asked about Phil Griffin, the president of MSNBC, or Comcast or Time Warner?"[150]

PLEASING THEIR BENEFACTORS

"Journalists are rarely instructed, 'Don't print anything about that,' or, 'Don't print that fact.' Rather they understand that they are expected to because they understand the interests of those they wish to placate or grow close to. If you behave you'll

---

149 *60 Minutes Rewind* interview.

150 Interview by Afshin Rattansi, Going Underground, RT, August 6, 2016, https://www.youtube.com/watch?v=1IfrNZfqGsQ.

be patted on the head and rewarded, and if you don't behave then you won't. It's that simple."[151]

SEX CASE SEXIER THAN AN ESPIONAGE CASE

"From a journalistic point of view, as the largest international espionage case against a publisher in history, it is a very sexy case, which the media has reasons to protest every day. But there is one thing that is still sexier than an espionage case and that's a sex case no matter how bogus."[152]

THROWING THE FIRST AMENDMENT IN THE BIN

"If we're talking about creating threats to small publishers to stop them publishing, the U.S. has lost its way. It has abrogated its founding traditions, it has thrown the First Amendment in the bin, because publishers must be free to publish."[153]

---

151 Julian Assange, with Jacob Appelbaum, Andy Müller-Maguhn, and Jérémie Zimmermann, *Cypherpunks: Freedom and the Future of the Internet*, OR Books, 2012, p. 124.

152 "We Are Drowning in Material," interview, *Spiegel International*, July 20, 2015.

153 *60 Minutes Rewind* interview.

HARD TO BE MORE CONTROVERSIAL THAN TRUMP

"From the point of view of an investigative journalist organization like WikiLeaks, the problem with the Trump campaign is it's actually hard for us to publish much more controversial material than what comes out of Donald Trump's mouth every second day. I mean that's a really strange reality for most of the media to be in."[154]

SOLIDARITY AGAINST BANK JULIUS BAER

"[Bank Julius Baer, the largest private Swiss banking concern] had been hiding assets in the Cayman Islands and minimizing its own taxes. . . . We released a number of secret trust records. This is not a sort of conventional banking operation—this is using the laws of the Cayman Islands and trust hiding to conceal assets of wealthy and powerful individuals. In response, Baer threatened to sue us [and got an injunction that temporarily shut down wikileaks.org]. . . . We pulled together a big team of around twenty-two different lawyers [from] eleven mainstream media organizations, professional journalist

---

154 "Julian Assange on Possible 'October Surprise' for Clinton,"
    Fox News, August 26, 2016, https://www.foxnews.com/politics/
    assange-blasts-media-for-politicization-of-election-campaign-in-fox-
    interviews.

unions, NGOs, Harvard, University of Texas, and our own four lawyers, and won the day under the First Amendment. . . . That was a big deal. I mean, the *New York Times* put our IP address in its editorial. CBS came in to support us. . . . There was a strong mutual interest."[155]

TO BE COMPLETELY IMPARTIAL IS TO BE AN IDIOT

"It was surprising to me that we were seen as such an impartial arbiter of the truth, which may speak well to what we have done. . . . To be completely impartial is to be an idiot. This would mean that we would have to treat the dust in the street the same as the lives of people who have been killed."[156]

LIVING UP TO THE NAME OF JOURNALISM

"We are creating a space behind us that permits a form of journalism which lives up to the name that journalism has always tried to establish for itself. We are creating that space because

---

155 "WikiSecrets," interview by Martin Smith, PBS Frontline, documentary aired May 24, 2011, https://wikileaks.org/WikiSecrets-JulianAssange-Full.html.

156 Raffi Khatchadourian, "No Secrets," *The New Yorker*, May 31, 2010, https://www.newyorker.com/magazine/2010/06/07/no-secrets.

we are taking on the criticism that comes from robust expo-
sure of powerful groups."[157]

BEING RESPONSIBLE TO THE PUBLIC AND THE HIS-
TORICAL RECORD

"It's not enough to produce accurate reporting, because if
political leadership won't let it out, what are you going to do?
Analysts must be responsible—not to political leadership [but]
to the public, and they must be responsible to the historical
record."[158]

PARTNERING FOR GREATER IMPACT

"We've partnered with twenty or so newspapers across the
world, to increase the total impact, including by encouraging
each one of these news organizations to be braver. It made
them braver, though it did not entirely work in the case of the
New York Times. For example, one of the stories we found in
the Afghan War Diary was from 'Task Force 373,' a U.S. Special

---

157 Carole Cadwalladr, "Julian Assange, Monk of the Online Age
who Thrives on Intellectual Battle," *The Guardian*, August
1, 2010, https://www.theguardian.com/media/2010/aug/01/
julian-assange-wikileaks-afghanistan.

158 Julian Assange, Talk at Oxford Union Society, via video link, January
23, 2013, https://www.youtube.com/watch?v=4vQNWYnQjUE.

Forces assassination squad. Task Force 373 is working its way down an assassination list of some two thousand people for Afghanistan . . . the Joint Priority Effects List, or JPEL. It's supposedly a kill or capture list. But you can see from the material that we released that about 50 percent of cases were just kill—there's no option to 'capture' when a drone drops a bomb on someone. And in some cases Task Force 373 killed innocents, including one case where they attacked a school and killed seven children and no bona fide targets, and attempted to cover the whole thing up. This discovery became the cover story for *Der Spiegel*. It became an article in the *Guardian*. A story was written for the *New York Times* by national security correspondent Eric Schmitt, and that story was killed."[159]

---

159 Obrist, "In Conversation with Julian Assange, Part I."

JUSTICE

When you are exposed to an unjust situation, rather than the pressure causing you to fold, the injustice in the pressure generates an anger that is sustaining.[160]

NO PUBLISHER PROSECUTED FOR ESPIONAGE

"There's a special set of rules for soldiers, for members of the State Department, who are disclosing classified information. There's not a set of rules for publishers disclosing classified information. There is the First Amendment, it covers the case, and there's been no precedent that I'm aware of in the past fifty years of prosecuting a publisher for espionage. It is just not done. Those are the rules: you do not do it."[161]

---

160 "Pardonnez-moi: L'interview de Julian Assange," interview by Darius Rochebin, Radio Television Suisse, March 16, 2015, https://www.youtube.com/watch?v=-jtveshuX_U.

161 *60 Minutes Rewind*, interview by Steve Croft, January 30, 2011, https://www.youtube.com/watch?v=Ubknv_CxSUY.

PROCESS IS THE PUNISHMENT

"The Obama administration, supported by varying degrees by its Western allies, in the last eight years has prosecuted and investigated more publishers and journalists under the Espionage Act than all previous presidencies combined. . . . What a number of these cases have in common is not simply that they are recent, or that they are conducted sometimes without any charge, or that there are abuses in the formal process, it is that a technique has been developed in the West where the process was clearly the punishment."[162]

MAGIC CIRCLE OF THE VIENNA CONVENTION

"Physically, of course, they [the British police] could come in anytime they like. They could smash the door down. So, why can't they do that? Well, because there is a magic circle around the embassy and this magic circle is something called the Vienna Convention. It's the convention, the international legal convention—actually the one adhered to the most in terms of international law—that specifies you cannot do that. What

---

162 Juan Pancorbo and Clara López Rubio, dirs., *Hacking Justice*, Mediasur-Inselfilm, 2017.

enforces that law? Is it the goodness of the heart of the prime minister, David Cameron? Obviously not."[163]

DEFENDING THOSE WE LOVE

"Every time we witness an injustice and do not act, we train our character to be passive in its presence and thereby eventually lose all ability to defend ourselves and those we love. In a modern economy it is impossible to seal oneself off from injustice. If we have brains or courage, then we are blessed and called on not to frit these qualities away, standing agape at the ideas of others, winning pissing contests, improving the efficiencies of the neocorporate state, or immersing ourselves in *obscuranta*, but rather to prove the vigor of our talents against the strongest opponents of love we can find."[164]

---

163 Tariq Ali and Margaret Kunstler, eds., *In Defense of Julian Assange*, OR Books, 2019, 174–175. The U.K. authorities, with the accord of the Ecuadorian government, which revoked Julian's asylum, did violate the "magic circle of the Vienna Convention," entering and dragging Julian out of the embassy on April 11, 2019, taking him to high-security Belmarsh Prison, where he remains.

164 Julian Assange, "Witnessing," from "Selected Correspondence," January 3, 2007, http://web.archive.org/web/20071020051936/http://iq.org/#Witnessing.

HOW FRANCE COULD SEND A MESSAGE

"In welcoming me, France would perform an act that is humanitarian but also probably symbolic, sending encouragement to all the journalists and whistleblowers throughout the world who risk their lives every day to bring their fellow citizens one step closer to the truth. France would also be sending a message to all those around the world who, seized by hubris, betray their values by incessantly attacking those citizens who refuse to do so."[165]

LOOKING TO OUR FEELINGS OF COMPASSION

"We must all look to ourselves and understand whether what we are doing is right and just, not just according to the views of our superiors but according to the long view

---

165 Julian Assange, letter addressed to President François Hollande, published in *Le Monde*, July 3, 2015, https://www.lemonde.fr/idees/article/2015/07/03/julian-assange-monsieur-hollande-accueillez-moi-en-france_4668919_3232.html. The French Minister of Justice and many others had proposed that President Hollande grant asylum to Julian, who had lived for a while in France and whose former partner and their child live there. This letter was published just days after WikiLeaks revealed that between 2006 and 2012 the U.S. National Security Agency had intercepted communications of three French presidents. Hollande refused to grant asylum to Julian.

of history, according to human rights and to our feelings of compassion."[166]

FOR THE CAUSE AND PURSUIT OF JUSTICE

The choices that we have made, that we make, is that we want to bring about a more just world, that we are interested in justice. That is the value of the organization. We say the way to get justice is through the Fourth Estate in general, to give democracy the lifeblood that it needs. So we look for and prioritize acts of injustice that expose abuse within the material we have, because we have limited resources. We are not in this to make money. We are not in this for political reasons. We are in this for the cause and pursuit of justice, and we are using a tried and true technique of getting justice, which is to expose injustice."[167]

BIG HOPE FOR THE BIG FUTURE

"There's the big future, there's the deep future, that one can long for. So that is a future where we are all able to freely

---

166   Julian Assange, Talk at Oxford Union Society, via video link, January 23, 2013, https://www.youtube.com/watch?v=4vQNWYnQjUE.

167   "WikiSecrets," interview by Martin Smith, PBS Frontline, documentary aired May 24, 2011, https://wikileaks.org/WikiSecrets-JulianAssange-Full.html.

communicate our hopes and dreams, and factual information about the world with each other, and the historical record is an item that is completely sacrosanct, that would never be changed, never be modified, never be deleted, and we will steer a course away from Orwell's dictum of 'he who controls the present controls the past.' So that is something that is my life-long quest to do. And from that, justice flows, because most of us have an instinct for justice, and most of us are reasonably intelligent, and if we can communicate with each other, organize, not be oppressed, and know what's going on, then pretty much the rest falls out. So, that is my big hope."[168]

ESPIONAGE INDICTMENT THE NEW PEACE PRIZE

"It is getting to the point where the mark of international distinction and service to humanity is no longer the Nobel Peace Prize, but an espionage indictment from the U.S. Department of Justice."[169]

---

168 Democracy Now at the Frontline Club, August 16, 2012, https://www.democracynow.org/2012/8/16/from_our_archives_full_video_of_wikileaks_julian_assange_philoso-pher_slavoj_iek_with_amy_goodman.

169 Statement by Julian Assange after One Year in Ecuadorian Embassy, June 22, 2013.

UNCEASING ATTACKS

"Listing the actions that have been directed against my organization, those close to me, and myself, fails to convey all the violence, but may give an idea: calls for my execution, for my kidnapping, and for my imprisonment on espionage charges by highly placed political and administrative leaders in the U.S.; theft of information, documents, and property; repeated cyber-attacks; continual infiltration; [an] illegal ban on the use of all payment platforms to make contributions to my organization; permanent surveillance of my every move and my electronic communications; indiscriminate legal prosecutions that have been dragged out for five years without the possibility of my being able to defend myself; slander campaigns; repeated physical threats; searches; and harassment of my lawyers, etc."[170]

EUROPEAN PARLIAMENT SUPPORT FOR WIKILEAKS AGAINST BANKING BLOCKADE

"I welcome this response from EU lawmakers. European independence is important. But there is no sovereignty without economic sovereignty. Politicized U.S. financial monopolies

170   Julian Assange, letter to Hollande, published in *Le Monde*, July 3, 2015.

must not be able to censor European organizations with impunity."[171]

TIME FOR FINE DEEDS, NOT FINE WORDS

"Fine words languish without commensurate actions. President Obama spoke out strongly in favour of the freedom of expression. 'Those in power,' he said, 'have to resist the temptation to crack down on dissent.' There are times for words and there are times for action. The time for words has run out. It is time for the U.S. to cease its persecution of WikiLeaks, to cease its

---

171 "European Parliament Votes to Protect WikiLeaks," November 20, 2012, https://wikileaks.org/European-Parliament-votes-to.html. In December 2010, Visa, Mastercard, PayPal, Western Union, and Bank of America launched a unilateral, extrajudicial, highly political banking blockade against donations to WikiLeaks. At that time the blockade had cost the organization more than US$50 million in donations. The U.S. Treasury formally found in 2011 that there was no lawful reason why WikiLeaks should be placed on the U.S. embargo list, but the blockade continued. In July of 2012, 95 percent of WikiLeaks' donations had been lost, costing the organization more than US$20 million, at which time WikiLeaks launched a new payment gateway for donations (see also fn. 92). On November 20, 2012, the European Parliament voted to draft legislation that would stop the arbitrary banking blockades against WikiLeaks and other organizations facing economic censorship, thereby underscoring WikiLeaks's claim that if the financial blockade against WikiLeaks were not stopped, U.S. financial giants would be free to unilaterally decide which European companies and organizations would live or die. (See also: "WikiLeaks Opens Path Through Banking Siege. Donations Open," July 18, 2012, https://wikileaks.org/Press-Release-WikiLeaks-opens-path.html).

persecution of our people, and to cease its persecution of our alleged sources. It is time for President Obama to do the right thing, and join the forces of change, not in fine words but in fine deeds."[172]

BRINGING JUSTICE TO THE JUSTICE SYSTEM

"Justice wasn't something that came out of the justice system. Justice was something that you bring to the justice system. And if you're lucky, or skilled, and you're in a country that isn't too corrupt, you can do that."[173]

EFFECTS OF MASS LEAKING

"The more secretive or unjust an organization is, the more leaks induce fear and paranoia in its leadership and planning coterie. This must result in minimization of efficient internal communications mechanisms (an increase in cognitive 'secrecy tax') and consequent system-wide cognitive

---

172 Address to the United Nations Human Rights Council (from the Ecuadorian embassy), September 27, 2012, https://wikileaks.org/Transcript-of-Julian-Assange.html.

173 Nikki Barrowclough, "The Secret Life of WikiLeaks Founder Julian Assange," *Sydney Morning Herald,* May 22, 2010, https://www.smh.com.au/technology/the-secret-life-of-wikileaks-founder-julian-assange-20100521-w1um.html.

decline resulting in decreased ability to hold onto power as the environment demands adaption. Hence in a world where leaking is easy, secretive or unjust systems are nonlinearly hit relative to open, just systems. Since unjust systems by their nature induce opponents, and in many places barely have the upper hand, mass leaking leaves them exquisitely vulnerable to those who seek to replace them with more open forms of governance. Only revealed injustice can be answered; for man to do anything intelligent he has to know what's actually going on."[174]

A SUPRANATIONAL ORGANIZATION

"We're interested in justice. We are a supranational organisation. So we're not interested in national security."[175]

EXERCISING INALIENABLE RIGHTS

"I speak to you today as a free man, because despite having been detained for 659 days without charge, I am free in the most basic and important sense. I am free to speak my mind.

---

174 Julian Assange, "The Non Linear Effects of Leaks on Unjust Systems of Governance," blog of December 31, 2006, http://cryptome. org/0002/ja-conspiracies.pdf.

175 Barrowclough, "Secret Life of Julian Assange."

This freedom exists because the nation of Ecuador has granted me political asylum and other nations have rallied to support its decision. And it is because of Article 19 of the United Nations Universal Declaration of Human Rights that WikiLeaks is able to 'receive and impart information . . . through any media, and any medium and regardless of frontiers'. It is thanks to the United Nations that I am able to exercise my inalienable right to seek protection from the arbitrary and excessive actions taken by governments against me and the staff and supporters of my organisation. It is because of the absolute prohibition on torture enshrined in customary international law and the UN Convention Against Torture that we stand firmly to denounce torture and war crimes, as an organisation, regardless of who the perpetrators are."[176]

CONSPIRACY TO COMMIT JOURNALISM

"We no longer need to comprehend the 'Kafkaesque' through the lens of fiction or allegory. It has left the pages and lives among us, stalking our best and brightest. It is fair to call what is happening to [Chelsea] Manning a 'show trial'. Those

---

176   Address to the United Nations Human Rights Council, September 27, 2012.

invested in what is called the 'U.S. military justice system' feel obliged to defend what is going on, but the rest of us are free to describe this travesty for what it is. No serious commentator has any confidence in a benign outcome. The pretrial hearings have comprehensively eliminated any meaningful uncertainty, inflicting pre-emptive bans on every defense argument that had any chance of success. . . . This is not justice; never could this be justice. The verdict was ordained long ago. Its function is not to determine questions such as guilt or innocence, or truth or falsehood. It is a public relations exercise, designed to provide the government with an alibi for posterity. It is a show of wasteful vengeance; a theatrical warning to people of conscience. The alleged act in respect of which [Chelsea] Manning is charged is an act of great conscience—the single most important disclosure of subjugated history, ever. There is not a political system anywhere on the earth that has not seen light as a result. In court, in February, [Chelsea] Manning said that [she] wanted to expose injustice and to provoke worldwide debate and reform. [Chelsea] Manning is accused of being a whistleblower . . . [she] is effectively accused of conspiracy to commit journalism."[177]

---

177 Assange Statement on the First Day of Manning Trial, June 3, 2013, https://wikileaks.org/Assange-Statement-on-the-First-Day.html.

DEALING WITH TRANSPARENCY

"Organizations really only have two choices to deal with transparency. The first choice is they can simply stop doing things that embarrass the public, so instead of committing an unjust act, commit a just act. Instead of hiding something, explain it. That's one choice. The other choice is that they can spend more on their security; they can become more baroque; they can take things off-record, speak orally and continue with this course of unjust action. But if they do that, they will become inefficient compared to other organizations, and they will shrink in their power and scale."[178]

---

178 "WikiSecrets" interview.

POWER

The greater the power, the more need there is for transparency, because if the power is abused, the result can be so enormous. On the other hand, those people who do not have power, we mustn't reduce their power even more by making them yet more transparent.[179]

UNDERSTANDING POWER

"I do have a political temperament, which is a combination of libertarianism and the importance of understanding. And what emerges from this temperament is holding power to account through action driven by understanding. So, if you have a libertarian temperament, then you're temperamentally opposed to authoritarian power. And if you have a temperament that is inclined to understanding, then you want to know what power is about. These two things combined drive forth

179 Decca Aitkenhead, "Julian Assange: The Fugitive," Guardian, December 7, 2012, https://www.theguardian.com/media/2012/dec/07/julian-assange-fugitive-interview.

a position, an intellectual and political position, that is about understanding power to such a degree that power is not able to express its most abusive aspects."[180]

OUTMANEUVERING INSTITUTIONAL DINOSAURS

"Institutional heads or political heads such as presidents spend most of the time trying to walk in front of the train and pretending that it is following them, but the direction is set by the tracks and by the engine of the train. Understanding that means that small and committed organisations can outmanoeuvre these institutional dinosaurs like the State Department, the NSA or the CIA."[181]

MOSTLY AN ILLUSION

"Power is mostly the illusion of power. The Pentagon demanded we destroy our publications. We kept publishing. Clinton denounced us and said we were an attack on the entire 'international community'. We kept publishing. I was put in prison and under house arrest. We kept publishing. We went head

---

180 "In Conversation with Julian Assange, Part II," Hans Ulrich Obrist, Journal #26, e-flux, June 2011, https://www.e-flux.com/journal/26/67921/in-conversation-with-julian-assange-part-ii/.

181 Stefania Maurizi, "Donald? It's a Change Anyway," *Republica*, December 23, 2016, https://www.repubblica.it/esteri/2016/12/23/news/assange_wikileaks-154754000/.

to head with the NSA getting Edward Snowden out of Hong Kong, we won and got him asylum. Clinton tried to destroy us and was herself destroyed. Elephants, it seems, can be brought down with string. Perhaps there are no elephants."[182]

UNACCOUNTABLE POWER IS SILENT

"Power that is completely unaccountable is silent. So, when you walk past a group of ants on the street and you accidentally crush a few, you do not turn to the others and say, 'Stop complaining, or I'll put a drone strike on your head.' You completely ignore them. And that is what happens to power that's in a very dominant position. It does not even bother to respond. It doesn't flinch for an instant."[183]

PUSHING BACK AGAINST POWERFUL LOBBIES

"We are a small organization that does not yet have a vast and powerful lobby to support it. But at the same time, we are taking on extremely powerful groups that do have vast and powerful lobbies to support them. So of course we are going

182 Ibid.

183 Democracy Now at the Frontline Club, August 16, 2012, https://www. democracynow.org/2012/8/16/ from_our_archives_full_video_of_ wikileaks_julian_assange_ philosopher_slavoj_iek_with_amy_goodman.

to be attacked in all sorts of manners. Of course people are going to try and capitalize and distort and hype up any sort of possible criticism. . . . On the other hand, actually, the people and young journalists and some very good older journalists are strongly supportive of us. And people are starting to see, as we're having this fight for political perception and for legitimacy in the public sphere, that actually we do have some people on our side."[184]

SPREADING TENTACLES OF THE PATRONAGE SYSTEM

"I see in the United States that there is now a rivalry between the modern form of the military industrial complex and Wall Street for this central [patronage] pyramid. And the military industrial complex has been broadening and expanding its share of that patronage system aggressively. There are now around nine hundred thousand people in the United States that have top-secret security clearances. Ten years ago, the National Security Agency dealt with about sixteen private contractors. The National Security Agency is the biggest spy agency in the

---

184 "WikiSecrets," interview by Martin Smith, PBS Frontline, documentary aired May 24, 2011, https://wikileaks.org/WikiSecrets-JulianAssange-Full.html.

United States, and its combined budget is more than that of the FBI and CIA combined, or at least it was around eight years ago when I had the last statistic. Now, it has over one thousand contractors. Similarly, U.S. involvement in Iraq created around ten thousand different private contractors. So the patronage is now moving into the private sector. It's less contained than it was. Its tentacles are spreading into all walks of our society and the number of people who are connected through family and business relationships, to that structure, continues to increase."[185]

THE BIRDS AND THE BEES

"The birds and the bees, and other things that can't actually change human power relationships, are free. They're left unmolested by human beings because they don't matter. In places where speech is free, and where censorship does not exist or is not obvious, the society is so sewn up—so depoliticized, so fiscalized in its basic power relationships—that it doesn't matter what you say. And it doesn't matter what information is published. It's not going to change who owns what or who

---

185 "In Conversation with Julian Assange, Part II."

controls what. And the power structure of a society is by definition its control structure."[186]

HYSTERIA FOLLOWING DISCLOSURES

"When WikiLeaks publishes U.S. government documents with classification markings—a type of national security 'holy seal,' if you will—two parallel campaigns begin: first, the public campaign of downplaying, diverting attention from, and reframing any revelations that are a threat to the prestige of the national security class; and second, an internal campaign within the national security state itself to digest what has happened. When documents carrying such seals are made public, they are transubstantiated into forbidden objects that become toxic to the 'state within a state'—the more than 5.1 million Americans (as of 2014) with active security clearances, and those on its extended periphery who aspire to its economic or social patronage. There is a level of hysteria and non-corporeality

---

186 "In Conversation with Julian Assange, Part I," Hans Ulrich Obrist, Journal #25, e-flux, May 2011, https://www.e-flux.com/journal/25/67875/in-conversation-with-julian-assange-part-i/.

exhibited in this reaction to WikiLeaks' disclosures that is not easily captured by traditional theories of power."[187]

CONSPIRACIES AS COGNITIVE DEVICES

"Conspiracies are cognitive devices. They are able to out-think the same group of individuals acting alone. Conspiracies take information about the world in which they operate (the conspiratorial environment), pass through the conspirators, and then act on the result. We can see conspiracies as a type of device that has inputs (information about the environment), a computational network (the conspirators and their links to each other), and outputs (actions intending to change or maintain the environment). . . . Since a conspiracy is a type of cognitive device that acts on information acquired from its environment, distorting or restricting these inputs means acts based on them are likely to be misplaced. Programmers call this effect 'garbage in, garbage out'. Usually the effect runs the other way; it is conspiracy that is the agent of deception and information restriction. In the U.S., the programmer's aphorism is sometimes called 'the Fox News effect'."[188]

---

187 WikiLeaks, with introduction by Julian Assange, *The WikiLeaks Files: The World According to U.S. Empire*, Verso, 2015, p. 6–7.

188 Julian Assange, "Conspiracies are Cognitive Devices," blog of December 3, 2006, http://cryptome.org/0002/ja-conspiracies.pdf.

PRISON

No state accepts to call the people it is imprisoning, or detaining for political reasons, political prisoners.[189]

ADAPTABILITY OF HUMANS

"One of the best attributes of human beings is that they are adaptable. One of the worst attributes of human beings is that they are adaptable. They adapt and start to tolerate abuses. They adapt to being themselves involved in abuses. They adapt to adversity and continue on. In my situation, frankly, I'm a bit institutionalized. This is the world, visually this is the world. It's a world without sunlight but I haven't seen sunlight in so long I don't remember it. You adapt. The one real irritant is that my young children, they also adapt, they adapt to being

189 "Secret World of U.S. Election: Julian Assange Talks to John Pilger," interview by John Pilger, Dartmouth Films, November 5, 2016, https://www.youtube.com/watch?v=_sbT3_9dJY4.

without their father. That's a hard adaption which they didn't ask for. I worry about them, I worry about their mother."[190]

SOLITARY REFLECTIONS

"During my time in solitary confinement in the bottom of a Victorian prison, I had time to reflect on the conditions of those people around the world also in solitary confinement, also on remand, in conditions that are more difficult than those faced by me."[191]

COST OF EMBASSY SURVEILLANCE

"This space is under permanent surveillance by several dozen British uniformed police who regularly check the identity of my visitors, and there are any number of plainclothes officers and intelligence agents within adjacent buildings. The cost

---

190 Ibid.

191 Andrew Fowler, *The Most Dangerous Man in the World: How One Hacker Ended Corporate and Government Secrecy Forever*, Skyhorse Publishing, 2013, p. 218. In December 2010 Julian spent a week in Wandsworth Prison in London whilst fighting to be released on bail in connection with the Swedish sexual assault allegations. He was released, under strict house arrest. Curiously (or not) his arrest coincided with major WikiLeaks publications: the Afghan War Logs five months earlier; the Iraq War Logs in October; Cablegate in November. This statement was made on the day of Julian's release, outside the prison.

of my surveillance has officially exceeded €15 million. This doesn't include the cost of the secret services."[192]

CALLING A POLITICAL PRISONER A POLITICAL PRISONER

"It doesn't suit the Western establishment narrative that, yes, the West has political prisoners. It's a reality, it's not just me, there's a bunch of other people as well. . . . No state accepts to call the people it is imprisoning, or detaining for political reasons, political prisoners. They don't call them political prisoners in China. They don't call them political prisoners in Azerbaijan. And they don't call them political prisoners in the U.S., U.K., or Sweden. It's absolutely intolerable to have that kind of self-perception."[193]

LIVING IN FIVE-AND-A-HALF SQUARE METERS

"I have five-and-a-half square meters for my private use. Access to open air, to sunlight, has been forbidden by the British authorities. So, too, the possibility of going to hospital. I have been able to use the balcony on the ground floor of the

---

192 Julian Assange, letter to Hollande, published in *Le Monde*, July 3, 2015.

193 "Secret World of U.S. Election."

apartment only three times since I took refuge here [to deliver public statements], at some personal risk, and I have never been allowed to go outside to exercise. The embassy of Ecuador, which honors me with its generosity and courage that have probably saved my life, is only an apartment used by a dozen diplomats and employees who can't abandon their mission. Far from the luxurious images associated with embassy interiors, Ecuador's is a very modest space, not meant to be lived in. For the past three years it has been impossible for me to have any kind of family or private life. . . . My youngest child and his mother are French. I haven't been able to see them for five years, since the beginning of my political persecution."[194]

THREE BOOKS, 5 MILLION DOCUMENTS PUBLISHED WHILE IN THE ECUADORIAN EMBASSY

"I came in here because I wanted to have a place where I could continue working. In prison I can't do that. And so I had upset the natural order of things. It's not an easy environment by any stretch of the imagination, but I'm not going to tell you how I'm suffering. That's boring. Actually, I have published three books in here, and more than 5 million documents. The

194 Assange, letter to Hollande.

organization continues to function, we have not been driven into bankruptcy, and we are now making our own prosecutions, not simply being prosecuted. This is quite disturbing to that perception of what the natural order of things is."[195]

LIGHT IS THE CUE

"There are people in much worse situations than I am in. There are also people in better situations. It just means that you need to be really diligent about dealing with it: trying to exercise; [dealing with] the lights because there's no sun, so you try and have lights going on at the right time of day and off at other times. It's like people working at the North Pole or in the space station. You have to deal with the absence of light. The light is the cue that sets your clock."[196]

ALL THE EMBASSY'S A STAGE

"If you think about it [asylum in the Ecuadorian embassy] from a theater or art perspective, it's not simply a matter of diplomatic law and political situation. Here we have some kind

---

195 Tariq Ali and Margaret Kunstler, eds., *In Defense of Julian Assange*, OR Books, 2019, p. 184.

196 Juan Pancorbo and Clara López Rubio, dirs., *Hacking Justice*, Mediasur-Inselfilm, 2017.

of stage. This embassy is a stage. It has an audience out front. It has actors—all those police, me, some extras, crowds that turn up. So what is the nature of the play? If you were a playwright, a theater director, how much would you pay for a stage like that? You would probably pay quite a lot for a stage with a guaranteed international audience. You can go out on that balcony and put on your show and draw attention to some particular artistic thought and have guaranteed attention."[197]

CUT OFF AND COUNTING ON OTHERS

"I have been isolated from all ability to prepare to defend myself: no laptop, no internet, ever, no computer, no library, so far, and even if I get access it will be just for half an hour, with everyone else, once a week. Just two visits a month and it takes weeks to get someone on the call list and a Catch-22 in getting their details to be security screened. Then all calls except [those with] lawyers are recorded, and calls are max ten minutes and in a limited thirty-minute window each day in which all prisoners compete for the phone. And credit? Just a few pounds a week and no one can call in. The other side? A superpower that has been preparing for nine years with

---

197   Ali and Kunstler, *In Defense of Julian Assange*, p. 186–187.

hundreds of people and untold millions spent on the case. I am defenseless and am counting on you and others of good character to save my life."[198]

---

198 Julian Assange, letter from Belmarsh Prison, published in *The Canary*, May 13, 2019, https://defend.wikileaks.org/2019/05/26/julian-assange-writes-a-letter-from-belmarsh-prison/. This letter was written one month after Julian was imprisoned in Belmarsh. He was first detained in solitary confinement until prisoners and his legal team protested, after which he was moved to a wing with forty other prisoners. When Covid-19 broke out shortly thereafter, affecting both prisoners and staff, the prison was placed in lockdown, with no visitors permitted for six months.

SOCIETY

You can't build a skyscraper out of Plasticine. And you can't build a just civilization out of ignorance and lies.[199]

SCALING HEIGHTS

"Intelligence and sadness may sometimes be correlated, but it seems far more in the application than in the possession, for while the mind is a rope to pull one out of the pit and those in it sometimes show it to desperate degree once free and on the surface, the same rope can also scale heights of love and accomplishment invisible from the narrow confines below."[200]

ROUSSEAUIAN VISION OF THE WORLD

"I had a Rousseauian vision of the world: that the way to make the world more just and interesting is for people to be better

---

199 Statement by Julian Assange after Six Months in Ecuadorian Embassy, December 20, 2012.

200 Julian Assange, "Pit and Pendulum," blog of July 17, 2006, http://web.archive.org/web/20061127092652/http://iq.org/.

educated. Because of the nature of its funding, the academy, universities, and formal schooling have developed along a certain line that tries to avoid conflict. Studying how human institutions actually behave in the modern world, especially examining how armies kill people, or how intelligence agencies corrupt other institutions, is not something the academy will ever touch as a result of its funding sources. . . . It will sometimes look at things if you go back fifty years or more because all those people studied are now out of power. You can learn some things from what happened fifty years ago, but really the world has been changing fast in this post-WWII period. To understand how the world works now you need to study what is happening now."[201]

WHERE YOU PUT YOUR MONEY IS WHERE YOU PUT YOUR POWER

"We all speak about the privacy of communication and the right to publish. That's something that's quite easy to understand—it has a long history—and, in fact, journalists love to talk about it because they're protecting their own interests. But if we compare that value to the value of the privacy and freedom of economic interaction, actually every time the

---

201 Ali and Kunstler, *In Defense of Julian Assange*, pp. 170–171.

CIA sees an economic interaction they can see that it's this party from this location to this party in this location, and they have a figure to the value and importance of the interaction. So isn't the freedom, or privacy, of economic interactions actually more important than the freedom of speech, because economic interactions really underpin the whole structure of society? . . . Where you put your money is where you put your power."[202]

PHILOSOPHY OF TECHNIQUE

"I'm quite interested in the philosophy of technique. Technique means not just a piece of technology but it means, say, majority consensus on a board, or the structure of a parliament—it's systematized interaction. For example, it seems to me that feudal systems came from the technique of mills. Once you had centralized mills, which required huge investments and which were easily subject to physical control, then it was quite natural that you would end up with feudal relations as a result. As time has gone by we seem to have developed increasingly

---

202 Julian Assange, with Jacob Appelbaum, Andy Müller-Maguhn, and Jérémie Zimmermann, *Cypherpunks: Freedom and the Future of the Internet*, OR Books, 2012, pp. 101–102.

sophisticated techniques. Some of these techniques can be democratized; they can be spread to everyone. But the majority of them—because of their complexity—are techniques that form as a result of strongly interconnected organizations like Intel Corporation. . . . I think that the general tendency for technique is to centralize control in those people who control the physical resources of techniques."[203]

BANKRUPTCY OF EXISTING POLITICAL THEORIES

"If we can find out about how complex human institutions actually behave, then we have a chance to build civilized behavior on top of it. This is why I say that all existing political theories are bankrupt, because you cannot build a meaningful theory without knowledge of the world that you're building the theory about. Until we have an understanding of how the world actually works, no political theory can actually be complete enough to demand a course of action."[204]

---

203 Ibid., p. 26.

204 "In Conversation with Julian Assange, Part I," Hans Ulrich Obrist, Journal #25, e-flux, May 2011, https://www.e-flux.com/journal/25/67875/in-conversation-with-julian-assange-part-i/.

THE RIGHT TO SPEAK COMES FROM OUR RIGHT TO KNOW

"What does it mean to have the right to speak if you're on the moon and there's no one around? It doesn't mean anything. Rather, the right to speak comes from our right to know. And the two of these together . . . produce a right to communicate, and so that is the grounding structure for all that we treasure about civilized life."[205]

DEMOCRATIZATION OF COMMUNICATION

"The future of humanity is the struggle between humans that control machines and machines that control humans; between the democratization of communication and usurpation of communication by artificial intelligence."[206]

LAYERS OF COMPLEXITY AND SECRECY

"Western societies specialize in laundering censorship and structuring the affairs of the powerful such that any remaining

---

205 Democracy Now at the Frontline Club, August 16, 2012, https://www.democracynow.org/2012/8/16/ from_ our_archives_full_video_of_wikileaks_julian_assange_ philosopher_slavoj_iek_with_amy_goodman.

206 Statement to the "Organizing Resistance to Internet Censorship" webinar organized by the World Socialist Website, January 16, 2018.

public speech that gets through has a hard time affecting the true power relationships of a highly fiscalized society, because such relationships are hidden in layers of complexity and secrecy."[207]

VISION OF A POSITIVE TRAJECTORY FOR THE FUTURE

"I posed the question of what the most positive trajectory for the future would look like. Self-knowledge, diversity, and networks of self-determination. A highly educated global population—I do not mean formal education, but highly educated in their understanding of how human civilization works at the political, industrial, scientific, and psychological levels—as a result of the free exchange of communication, also stimulating vibrant new cultures and the maximal diversification of individual thought, increased regional self-determination, and the self-determination of interest groups that are able to network quickly and exchange value rapidly over geographic boundaries."[208]

ONLY A HIGH-TECH REBEL ELITE WILL REMAIN FREE

"The negative trajectory [is] a transnational surveillance state, drone-riddled, the networked neo-feudalism of the

207 Assange, *Cypherpunks,* p. 124.
208 Ibid, p. 157.

transnational elite. . . . How can a normal person be free within that system? They simply cannot, it's impossible. Not that anyone can ever be completely free, within any system, but the freedoms that we have biologically evolved for, and the freedoms that we have become culturally accustomed to, will be almost entirely eliminated. So I think the only people who will be able to keep the freedom that we had, say twenty years ago—because the surveillance state has already eliminated quite a lot of that, we just don't realize it yet—are those who are highly educated in the internals of this system. So it will only be a high-tech rebel elite that is free."[209]

PLASTICINE VS PLATONIC

"We build all of our civilization, other than on bricks, on human intellectual content. We currently have a system with URLs where the structure we are building our civilization on is the worst kind of melting Plasticine imaginable. That's a big problem. . . . On the one hand you have live dynamic services and organizations that run those services—meaning a hierarchy, a system of control, be it an organization, a government, or some controlling group. And on the other hand you have human intellectual artifacts that can

---

209 Ibid., pp. 160–161.

be completely independent from any system of human control. They are out there in the Platonic realm. They should be referred to in a way that is intrinsic to their intellectual content, and not in a way that is dependent on an organization. I think that is an inevitable and very important way forward."[210]

LIVING OFF THE INTELLECTUAL RECORD

"We as human beings shepherd and create our intellectual history as a civilization. And it is that intellectual history on the shelf that we can pull off the shelf to do stuff, and to avoid doing the dumb things again, because somebody already did the dumb thing and wrote about their experience and we don't need to do it again. There are several different processes that are creating that record, and other processes where people are trying to destroy bits of that record, and others that are trying to prevent people from putting things into that record in the first place. We all live off that intellectual record. So what we want to do is get as much into the record, prevent as much as possible being deleted from the record, and then make the record as searchable as possible."[211]

---

210 Julian Assange, *When Google Met WikiLeaks*, New York, NY: OR Books, 2014, pp. 80–81.

211 Ibid., p. 124.

USING THE TIME WE HAVE

"We all only live once. So we are obligated to make good use of the time that we have and to do something that is meaningful and satisfying. This is something that I find meaningful and satisfying. That is my temperament. I enjoy creating systems on a grand scale, and I enjoy helping people who are vulnerable. And I enjoy crushing bastards. So it is enjoyable work."[212]

TRUE INTELLECTUAL HERITAGE

"[The whole point of free software is to] liberate it in all senses. . . . It's part of the intellectual heritage of man. True intellectual heritage can't be bound up in intellectual property."[213]

---

212 "WikiLeaks Founder Julian Assange on the 'War Logs': 'I Enjoy Crushing Bastards,'" interview by John Goetz and Marcel Rosenbach, *Spiegel International,* July 26, 2010, https://www.spiegel.de/international/world/wikileaks-founder-julian-assange-on-the-war-logs-i-enjoy-crushing-bastards-a-708518.html.

213 Nikki Barrowclough, "The Secret Life of WikiLeaks Founder Julian Assange," *Sydney Morning Herald*, May 22, 2010, https://www.smh.com.au/technology/the-secret-life-of-wikileaks-founder-julian-assange-20100521-w1um.html.

SURVEILLANCE

We are all living under martial law as far as our communications are concerned, we just can't see the tanks—but they are there.[214]

GLOBAL TOTALITARIAN SURVEILLANCE SOCIETY

"The natural efficiencies of surveillance technologies compared to the number of human beings will mean that slowly we will end up in a global totalitarian surveillance society—by totalitarian I mean a total surveillance—and that perhaps there will just be the last free living people, those who understand how to use this cryptography to defend against this complete, total surveillance, and some people who are completely off-grid, neo-Luddites that have gone into the cave, or traditional tribes-people who have none of the efficiencies of a modern economy and so their ability to act is very small. Of course anyone can stay off the

---

214 Julian Assange, with Jacob Appelbaum, Andy Müller-Maguhn, and Jérémie Zimmermann, *Cypherpunks: Freedom and the Future of the Internet*, OR Books, 2012, p. 33.

internet, but then it's hard for them to have any influence. They select themselves out of being influential by doing that. It's the same with mobile phones; you can choose not to have a mobile phone but you reduce your influence. It's not a way forward."[215]

PRIVACY TO PRESERVE POWER

"I have often said transparency for the powerful, privacy for the powerless. But who cares about privacy? There are some basic, instinctual notions of privacy—affairs between lovers, or when you go to the toilet. . . . It's actually a human instinct. But if we look beyond that, no one gives a damn about privacy. What people care about is power, and the relative balance of power between small organizations, the smallest of which is the family, and large organizations. However, information is power and if a large organization has a lot of information about you, and you don't have information about that organization, it has even more power over you than it otherwise would have. Privacy is a way for individuals and small organizations to preserve the small amount of power that they already have."[216]

---

215 Ibid., pp. 62–63.

216 Juan Pancorbo and Clara López Rubio, dirs., *Hacking Justice*, Mediasur-Inselfilm, 2017.

LIKE HAVING A TANK IN YOUR BEDROOM

"I see that there is now a militarization of cyberspace, in the sense of a military occupation. When you communicate over the internet, when you communicate using mobile phones, which are now meshed to the internet, your communications are being intercepted by military intelligence organizations. It's like having a tank in your bedroom. It's a soldier between you and your wife as you're SMSing. We're all living under martial law as far as our communications are concerned, we just can't see the tanks—but they are there. To that degree, the internet, which was supposed to be a civilian space, has become a militarized space. But the internet is our space, because we all use it to communicate with each other and with the members of our family. The communications at the inner core of our private lives now move over the internet. So in fact our private lives have entered into a militarized zone. It is like having a soldier under the bed. This is a militarization of civilian life."[217]

---

217 Assange, *Cypherpunks*, p. 33.

HOT PHONE TIP

"If you think you have a hot phone, you charge the battery up fully, and then you post it overseas."[218]

A WEAPON OF MASS DESTRUCTION

"I want to explore this analogy of mass surveillance being a weapon of mass destruction. . . .

With the increase in the sophistication and the reduction of the cost of bulk surveillance that has happened over the past ten years, we're now at a stage where the human population is doubling every twenty-five years or so—but the capacity of surveillance is doubling every eighteen months. The surveillance curve is dominating the population curve. There is no direct escape. We're now at the stage where just $10 million can buy you a unit to permanently store the mass intercepts of a medium sized country. So I wonder if we need an equivalent response. This really is a big threat to democracy and to freedom all around the world that needs a response, like the threat

---

218 Andrew Fowler, *The Most Dangerous Man in the World: How One Hacker Ended Corporate and Government Secrecy Forever*, New York, NY: Skyhorse Publishing, 2013, p. 154.

of atomic war needed a mass response, to try and control it, while we still can."[219]

DEFINING THE PROFILE OF AN INDIVIDUAL

"One speaks of espionage of mail or SMS, but one thing that isn't often remarked on and that should be observed is Visa and Mastercard. All the transactions they've collected and turned over to the CIA and NSA define the social and economic profile of the individual."[220]

GUIDE FOR THE EGYPTIAN REVOLUTION: DO NOT USE TWITTER OR FACEBOOK

"There is an idea that these great American companies, Facebook and Twitter, gave the Egyptian people this revolution and liberated Egypt. But the most popular guide for the revolutionaries was a document that spread throughout the soccer clubs in Egypt, which themselves were the most significant revolutionary community groups. If you read this document, you see that on the first page it says to be careful not to use Twitter and Facebook as they are being monitored. On the last page: do not

---

219 Assange, *Cypherpunks*, pp. 46–47.

220 "Pardonnez-moi," interview, Radio Television Suisse, March 16, 2015.

use Twitter or Facebook. That is the most popular guide for the Egyptian revolution."[221]

GREATEST THEFT OF INFORMATION

"[Surveillance] is the greatest theft of information that has ever happened—from every single one of us who uses the internet into the bowels of secret agencies. Now, if those secret agencies were working on our behalf perhaps we could accept it. If, as soon as possible, that material would enter into the historical record, would enter into the record of our civilization, where we could all individually make decisions using that information to produce a better, more harmonious world, then perhaps it would be tolerable, but it is not tolerable in its current form."[222]

---

221 "In Conversation with Julian Assange, Part I," Hans Ulrich Obrist, Journal #25, e-flux, May 2011, https://www.e-flux.com/journal/25/67875/in-conversation-with-julian-assange-part-i/.

222 Julian Assange, Talk at Oxford Union Society, via video link, January 23, 2013, https://www.youtube.com/watch?v=4vQNWYnQjUE.

WAR

Populations basically don't like wars and they have to be lied into it. That means we can be 'truthed' into peace.[223]

PERFECT RECORD OF PROTECTING SOURCES

"We are appalled that the U.S. military was so lackadaisical with its Afghan sources. Just appalled. We are a source protection organisation that specialises in protecting sources, and have a perfect record from our activities."[224]

AFGHAN WAR DIARIES SHIFTING PERCEPTION

"The Afghan War Diaries, which revealed ninety thousand different significant acts in Afghanistan, down to the meter, where they occurred, the particular locations involved, the deaths of

---

223 Julian Assange, *When Google Met WikiLeaks*, New York, NY: OR Books, 2014, p. 127.

224 Carole Cadwalladr, "Julian Assange, Monk of the Online Age who Thrives on Intellectual Battle," *The Guardian*, August 1, 2010, https://www.theguardian.com/media/2010/aug/01/julian-assange-wikileaks-afghanistan.

twenty thousand different people, individually recorded—that changed the perception of the Afghan War in 2010 irrevocably. We went from a situation where there was a discussion in early 2010 on whether more troops were needed and [whether] the United States [was] winning the war in Afghanistan or not. Post the revelations of the Afghan War Logs, the discussion was no longer that. The discussion was how can we get out, that it is a debacle, a quagmire . . . and the discussion since that point has always been how can we get out. A very important shift in perception of that war."[225]

LIED INTO WAR, TRUTHED INTO PEACE

"Most wars in the twentieth century started as a result of lies amplified and spread by the mainstream press. And you may say, 'Well that is a horrible circumstance; it is terrible that all these wars start with lies.' And I say no, this is a tremendous opportunity, because it means that populations basically don't like wars and they have to be lied into it. That means we can be 'truthed' into peace. This is cause for hope."[226]

---

225 "The Effect of the Afghan War Diaries," TheWikiLeaksChannel, June 24, 2019, https://www.youtube.com/watch?v=FQ7zrj14JfY.

226 Assange, *When Google Met WikiLeaks*, pp. 126–127.

LARGEST HISTORY OF A WAR

"[The Iraq War Logs were] the largest history of a war, the most detailed significant history of a war to have ever been published, probably at all, but definitely during the course of a war. . . . It provided a picture of the everyday squalor of war, from children being killed at roadside blocks, to over a thousand people being handed over to the Iraqi police for torture, to the reality of close-air support and how modern military combat is done."[227]

STORIES OF FIFTEEN THOUSAND IRAQI CIVILIANS KILLED

"We worked together . . . to pull out the stories of fifteen thousand Iraqi civilians, labeled as civilians by the U.S. military, who were killed, who were never before reported in the Iraqi press, never before reported in the U.S. press or in the world press, even in aggregate, even saying, 'Today a thousand people died'—not reported in any manner whatsoever. And you just think about that: fifteen thousand people whose deaths were

---

227 Democracy Now at the Frontline Club, August 16, 2012, https://www. democracynow.org/2012/8/16/from_our_archives_full_video_of_ wikileaks_julian_assange_ philosopher_slavoj_iek_with_amy_goodman.

recorded by the U.S. military but were completely unknown to the rest of the world. That's a very significant thing. And compare that to the three thousand people who died on 9/11. Imagine the significance for Iraqis."[228]

ANNEXATION BY DRONE OR ELECTRONIC INCURSION

"On a basic human level, the more one dehumanizes war and assassination, the more will occur. At a more philosophical level it's the breakdown of the concept of sovereignty, of borders, because it's very easy to send small drones across a border. It's like when the American National Security Agency enters into the computer system of Switzerland, it's an annexation of their territory—it's an annexation that happens in the computer world. The creeping annexation that is occurring in the electronic realm has its physical equivalent in drones. The drones are always smaller, very difficult to spot, very difficult to identify their origin. . . . The surveillance drones in the army can even be used for attacks."[229]

---

228 Democracy Now at the Frontline Club.

229 "Pardonnez-moi: L'interview de Julian Assange," interview by Darius Rochebin, Radio Television Suisse, March 16, 2015, https://www.youtube.com/watch?v=-jtveshuX_U.

CALLING COLLATERAL MURDER WHAT IT IS

"I wanted to call it [the Collateral Murder video] 'Permission to Engage,' because that was a phrase that came out of it. But that phrase was already used elsewhere. . . . And actually, we did want to attract attention to the very specific event of this journalist crawling in the gutter and being deliberately targeted and killed, even though he was unarmed, [along with] his rescuers. In common parlance, that is murder, and there is no doubt about it. We also released the rules of engagement, in very detailed description, including flow charts, to show that even under the U.S. military's internal procedure, that was not a justified attack. And all sorts of rhetoric occurred by a military apologist after the event, talking about, 'Oh, well, the rules of engagement perhaps allow this.' But we produced the rules of engagement. Not one of those people read those rules of engagement and said, 'Here, under this section, this is not a murder.' We did. I did. I am confident that that title is correct. . . . The way that this footage has [been circulated] in the world is effective. So there are continual documentaries and investigative reports that use this footage in many languages, in many nationalities. It is now part of the historical record."[230]

AFGHAN WAR LOGS CHANGING OUR PERSPECTIVE ON ALL WARS

"These files are the most comprehensive description of a war to be published during the course of a war—in other words, at a time when they still have a chance of doing some good. They cover more than ninety thousand different incidents, together with precise geographical locations. They cover the small and the large. A single body of information, they eclipse all that has been previously said about Afghanistan. They will change our perspective on not only the war in Afghanistan, but on all modern wars. . . . There is a mood to end the war in Afghanistan. This information won't do it alone, but it will shift political will in a significant manner."[231]

---

230 "WikiSecrets," interview by Martin Smith, PBS Frontline, documentary aired May 24, 2011, https://wikileaks.org/WikiSecrets-JulianAssange-Full.html.

231 "Julian Assange on the 'War Logs,'" interview, *Spiegel International*, July 26, 2010.

PUBLISHING THE GOOD AND THE BAD

"We publish full information, pristine archives, verifiable. That often makes it inconvenient for propaganda purposes, because for many organisations you see the good and the bad, and that makes the facts revealed harder to spin. If we go back to the Iraq War in 2003, let's imagine U.S. intelligence tried to leak us some of their internal reports on Iraq. Now we know from U.S. intelligence reports that subsequently came out that there was internal doubt and scepticism about the claim that there were weapons of mass destruction in Iraq. Even though there was intense pressure on the intelligence services at the political level to create reports that supported the rush towards the war, internally their analysts were hedging. . . . If WikiLeaks had published those reports, these doubts would have been expressed and the war possibly averted."[232]

BOG-STANDARD TACTIC OF THE PENTAGON

"Whenever they are or expect to be criticized for slaying innocent civilians, thousands—in the case of the Afghan War

---

232 Stefania Maurizi, "Donald? It's a Change Anyway," *Republica*, December 23, 2016, https://www.republica.it/esteri/2016/12/23/ news/assange_wikileaks-154754000/.

Diaries—of people killed in this conflict, over twenty thousand documented in our material—whenever they come under that criticism, they use the bog-standard rhetorical trick which is to turn the precise criticism that you expect back on your opponent. So the criticism that they were expecting is they were involved in the situation that has led to the deaths. . . . So what do they say? They say we [WikiLeaks] might have blood on our hands, when their own records document that broader military conflict killing twenty thousand people."[233]

---

233 "WikiSecrets" interview.

WIKILEAKS

We are, if you like, enforcing the First Amendment around the world.[234]

THREAT TO WIKILEAKS IS THREAT TO ALL

"As WikiLeaks stands under threat, so does the freedom of expression and the health of our societies. We must use this moment to articulate the choice that is before the government of the United States of America. Will it return to and reaffirm the values it was founded on, or will it lurch off the precipice dragging us all into a dangerous and oppressive world, in which journalists fall silent under the fear of prosecution and citizens must whisper in the dark? I say that it must turn back."[235]

---

234 Andrew Fowler, *The Most Dangerous Man in the World: How One Hacker Ended Corporate and Government Secrecy Forever*, New York, NY: Skyhorse Publishing, 2013, p. xiii.

235 Official Statement by Julian Assange from the Ecuadorian Embassy, August 19, 2012.

REBEL LIBRARY OF ALEXANDRIA

"WikiLeaks has become the rebel library of Alexandria. It is the single most significant collection of information that doesn't exist elsewhere, in a searchable, accessible, citable form, about how modern institutions actually behave. And it's gone on to set people free from prison, where documents have been used in their court cases; hold the CIA accountable for renditions programs; [and] feed into election cycles. . . . Our civilization can only be as good as our knowledge of what our civilization is. We can't possibly hope to reform that which we do not understand."[236]

STICKING TO OUR PUBLISHING PROMISE

"We don't go after a particular country, we don't go after a particular organizational group. We just stick to our promise of publishing material that is likely to have a significant impact."[237]

---

236 "Julian Assange: Choosing between Trump or Clinton is Like Picking between Cholera or Gonorrhea," Democracy Now interview Part 2, July 25, 2016.

237 *60 Minutes Rewind*, interview by Steve Croft, January 30, 2011, https://www.youtube.com/watch?v=Ubknv_CxSUY.

OUR FOUNDING VALUES

"Our founding values are those of the U.S. Revolution. They are those of people like Jefferson and Madison."[238]

PROMISE TO SOURCES

"The promise that we make to our sources is not only will we defend them through every means that we have available, technological and legally and politically, but we will try and get the maximum possible political impact for the material that they give to us."[239]

STARTING WITH OBSERVATIONS

"In the theory of change I outlined, we have a starting point. We have some observations about reality, like Kroll [an international private intelligence agency] observing where Daniel arap Moi [former president of Kenya] stashed all his money. Then that information came to us, and then we spread it around in a way designed to maximize impact. And it entered the minds of many people, and caused them to act. The result

---

238 Ibid.

239 Fowler, *The Most Dangerous Man in the World,* pp. 114–115.

was a change in the Kenyan election, which then went on to produce many other changes."[240]

JUSTICE PRODUCED BY THE FOURTH ESTATE

"We can look at this whole process as justice produced by the Fourth Estate. This description, which is partly derived from my experiences in quantum mechanics, looks at the flow of particular types of information which will effect some change in the end. The bottleneck appeared to me to be primarily in the acquisition of information that would go on to produce changes that were just. In a Fourth Estate context, the people who acquire information are sources; the people who work on information and distribute it are journalists and publishers; and the people who may act on it includes everyone. That's a high-level construct, but it then comes down to how you practically engineer a system that solves that problem, and not just a technical system but a total system. WikiLeaks was, and is, an attempt—although still very young—at a total system."[241]

---

240 "In Conversation with Julian Assange, Part I," Hans Ulrich Obrist, Journal #25, e-flux, May 2011, https://www.e-flux.com/journal/25/67875/in-conversation-with-julian-assange-part-i/.

241 Julian Assange, *When Google Met WikiLeaks*, New York, NY: OR Books, 2014, pp. 68–69.

BURNING SOURCES

"Most of the media organizations do burn sources. Edward Snowden was abandoned in Hong Kong, especially by the *Guardian*, which had run his stories exclusively. But we thought that it was very important that a star source like Edward Snowden was not put in prison. Because that would have created a tremendous chilling effect on other sources coming forward."[242]

FROM THE TOP INTO THE PUBLIC RECORD

"Most of the transfer of information has come from the bottom to these powerful intelligence organizations like Google and Facebook. WikiLeaks does it the other way. We take information from very powerful organizations, the most powerful organizations, and we put it in the public record where everyone can use it. That's unusual."[243]

---

242 "We Are Drowning in Material," interview, *Spiegel International*, July 20, 2015.

243 Juan Pancorbo and Clara López Rubio, dirs., *Hacking Justice*, Mediasur-Inselfilm, 2017.

CHANGING WASHINGTON'S BEHAVIOR TOWARD MUBARAK

"[In 2011, Joe Biden] said that Mubarak was not a dictator, but presumably a democrat, and that he should not stand down. Look at how the behavior of Washington changed with regard to Mubarak just before he fell. After we released these cables about the relationship between the United States and Mubarak in foreign military subsidies and the FBI's training of torturers in Egypt, it was no longer possible for Biden to make these kinds of statements. It became completely impossible, because their own ambassadors were saying, just the year before, that Suleiman and Mubarak had been extremely abusive to the Egyptian people in so many ways—and that the United States had been involved in that abuse, in some way."[244]

GIVING PEOPLE A CHOICE

"We are giving people a choice. If you have information about how the world is working around you, then you have a choice about what you support, what you don't support, what you do with your life."[245]

---

244 Obrist, "In Conversation with Julian Assange, Part I."

245 Pancorbo and López Rubio, *Hacking Justice*.

THE BIGGEST DOG IN THE ROOM

"WikiLeaks has published over 2 million diplomatic cables. It is the single largest repository for international relations of primary source materials, all searchable. It is the canon for international relations. It is the biggest dog in the room."[246]

SHADOW OF THE SHADOW

"People talk about WikiLeaks and they say, 'Look, all that private government information is now public, the government can't keep anything secret.' I say this is rubbish. I say that WikiLeaks is the shadow of a shadow. In fact, that we have produced over a million words of information and given it to the public is a function of the enormous explosion in the amount of secret material out there. And, in fact, powerful groups have such a vast amount of secret material now that it dwarfs the amount of publicly available material, and the operations of WikiLeaks are just a percentage fraction of this privately held material. When you look at this balance between powerful insiders knowing every credit card transaction in the world on the one hand, and on the other hand people being able to

---

246 "We Are Drowning in Material" interview.

Google and search for the blogs of the world and people's comments, how do you see this balance?"[247]

ILLEGITIMATE AUTHORITY ENCOURAGES WHISTLEBLOWERS

"[Chelsea Manning's sentencing] was designed to be a very strong deterrent. However, a number of people have come forward subsequent to that and these acts of repression have a mixed effect. Obviously, sentencing someone to thirty-five years in prison does have some deterrent effect. But it also erodes the perception of the U.S. Government as a legitimate authority. Being perceived as a just authority is the key to legitimacy. Edward Snowden told me they had abused Manning in a way that contributed to [Manning's] decision to become a whistleblower, because it shows the system is incapable of reforming itself."[248]

---

247 Julian Assange, with Jacob Appelbaum, Andy Müller-Maguhn, and Jérémie Zimmermann, *Cypherpunks: Freedom and the Future of the Internet*, OR Books, 2012, p. 145.

248 "We Are Drowning in Material" interview.

ATTACKING WIKILEAKS, IGNORING GOVERNMENT CRIMES

"It's interesting how some politicians single out my staff and myself for attack while saying nothing about the slaughter of thousands by the U.S. military or other dictatorships. It is cowardly to bully a small media organization, but that is what is happening here."[249]

SCIENTIFIC METHOD

"Everything we do is like science. It is checkable, independently checkable, because the information which has informed our conclusion is there. Just like scientific papers which are based on experimental data must make their experimental data available to other scientists and to the public, if they want their papers to be published. It's our philosophy that raw source material must be made available so that conclusions can be checkable."[250]

---

249 Fowler, *The Most Dangerous Man in the World*, p. 216.

250 Julian Assange, Talk at University of California at Berkeley, April 18, 2010, transcript https://zunguzungu.wordpress.com/2010/12/12/julian-assange-in-berkeley/.

LEARNING SOMETHING FROM THE MULTINATIONALS

"If you look at how multinational organizations move their tax structuring through offshore jurisdictions or just through trusts within countries like the U.K., we have to do the same thing in order to protect our sources [from] malicious, vexatious lawsuits affecting our ability to continue."[251]

CRITICAL OF RUSSIA, TOO

"We have published over eight hundred thousand documents, of various kinds, that relate to Russia. Most of those are critical. A great many books have come out of our publications about Russia, most of which are critical, and our documents have gone on to be used in quite a number of court cases, refugee cases, of people fleeing some kinds of claimed political persecution in Russia, which they use our documents to back up."[252]

---

251   Fowler, *The Most Dangerous Man in the World*, p. 97.

252   "The Secret World of US Election: Julian Assange talks to John Pilger," Dartmouth Films, November 5, 2016, https:// www.youtube.com/ watch?v=_sbT3_9dJY4.

PROMISING SOURCES IMPACT

"We promised our sources impact and we were delivering. If people were going to prison it would not be for nothing."[253]

PUBLISHING MORE AND FASTER BECAUSE OF FUND-ING SOURCES

"WikiLeaks is a global media organization. We are funded by the public. We're not funded by dodgy foundations. We're not funded by dodgy advertisers. We're funded by the public—in fact, mostly the American public. In fact we're tax deductible in the United States. You can go to wikileaks.org and hit the donate button. And that means we can publish more and we can publish faster."[254]

PRESERVING POLITICALLY SALIENT INTELLECTUAL CONTENT

"The issue of preserving politically salient intellectual content while it is under attack is central to what WikiLeaks does, because that's what we are after. We're after those bits

---

253 Assange, *When Google Met WikiLeaks,* p. 16.

254 "Julian Assange on Possible 'October Surprise' for Clinton," Fox News, August 26, 2016, 2016, https://www.foxnews.com/politics/ assange-blasts-media-for-politicization-of-election-campaign-in-fox-interviews.

that people are trying to suppress because we suspect, usually rightly, that they're expending economic work on suppressing those bits because they perceive that those bits are going to induce some change."[255]

COLLATERAL MURDER RELEASES HARMED NO ONE

"We have a clear result. The U.S. government had to admit in court under oath in 2013 that not a single person that it could find had been harmed as a result of our [Collateral Murder] disclosures."[256]

ONLY DEFENSES WERE TECHNICAL

"Initially WikiLeaks . . . didn't have significant political allies and we didn't have a worldwide audience that was looking to see how we were doing. So we took the position that we would need to have a publishing system where the only defense was anonymity. It had no financial defense; it had no legal defense; and it had no political defense. Its defenses were purely technical."[257]

---

255 Assange, *When Google Met WikiLeaks,* p. 83.

256 "Julian Assange Talks 'Revealing the Truth' Through WikiLeaks," Fox News, August 25, 2016, https://www.youtube.com/watch?v=_rLeuydV1xM.

257 Assange, *When Google Met WikiLeaks,* p. 71.

POWER OF TUNISIAN CABLES

"The Tunisian government concurrently banned *Al Akhbar* and WikiLeaks. Then, computer hackers who were sympathetic to us came and redirected the Tunisian government's own websites to us. There's one particular cable about Ben Ali's regime that covers his sort of internal, personal opulence and abuse, the abuse of proceeds. . . . Some people have reported that the people in Tunisia were very upset to hear about these abuses in this cable, and that inspired them to revolt. Some parts of that may be true, though two weeks later there was also a man who set himself on fire, the twenty-six-year-old computer technician, reportedly because of a dispute over a license in the market. And this took the rage to the streets. But my suspicion is that one of the real differences in the cables about Tunisia came in showing that the United States, if push came to shove, would support the army over Ben Ali. That was a signal, not just to the army, but to the other actors inside Tunisia, as well as to the surrounding states who might have been considering intervening with their intelligence services or military on behalf of Ben Ali."[258]

---

258 Obrist, "In Conversation with Julian Assange, Part I,"

VERIFYING DOCUMENTS, NOT SOURCES

"We don't verify sources; we verify that documents are official documents."[259]

CABLEGATE REVELATIONS USED IN COURT CASES

"[We can] see that corruption runs all the way from corrupt ticket inspectors to corruption at the geopolitical level, where false claims are made by a state's leadership in order to justify the invasion and destruction of another state. We've published a lot about corruption. Corruption hidden by secrecy and corruption hidden by complexity. According to Google, there are more than 1.5 million web pages on WikiLeaks' corruption revelations. Cablegate revelations have been used in many court cases from the International Criminal Court (the ICC) to domestic appeals courts. The most recent has been running since July and involves geopolitical corruption in which the U.K. government deported the entire native population of the Chagos Islands, turned it into a secret U.S. military base, Diego Garcia, and then conspired with the U.S. to falsely declare it a

---

259 Assange, *When Google Met WikiLeaks*, p. 178.

marine [reserve] to prevent the native population from claiming a right of return."[260]

CONTINGENCY PLANS

"We have contingency plans that you have seen in action when my internet was cut off and while I was in prison before. An organisation like WikiLeaks cannot be structured such that a single person can be a point of failure in the organization—it makes him or her a target."[261]

---

260 "Julian Assange Presentation to EU Parliament on Corruption Revealed in Cablegate," December 5, 2012, https://wikileaks.org/ Julian-Assange-Presentation-to-EU.html. The U.K. government attempted not to testify in the Chagos case, saying, "My clients are not opposing cross-examination because they have anything to hide. We are opposing it because, as a matter of principle, it does not seem right in relation to an improperly leaked document. We, as a matter of principle, do not accept that WikiLeaks can effectively compel the Government to defend something which— absent WikiLeaks—there would be no question of it coming before the court at all." The judge disagreed, ruling, "I do not see how the present claim can be fairly or justly determined without resolving the allegation made by the claimant, based on the WikiLeaks documents." (ibid.)

261 Stefania Maurizi, "Donald? It's a Change Anyway," *Republica*, December 23, 2016, https://www.repubblica.it/esteri/2016/12/23/ news/assange_wikileaks-154754000/.

DIGITAL TOOLS MEAN BETTER PREPARATION FOR COVID-19

"At the very least, transnational organisations like WikiLeaks and DiEM25 had honed the digital tools for online debates and campaigns well before Covid-19 came on the scene. In some measure, we are better prepared than others."[262]

AD HOMINEM ONLY WAY TO ATTACK

"Ad hominem attacks on the organization are directed at its front men. Yet through this mechanism of attracting attacks, we do keep those attacks away from people who are less able to respond to, deal with, or defend themselves against them. This also creates a sort of market that stems the likelihood of others being swept up into ad hominem attacks—simply because our publishing activities consist of putting out information that cannot be attacked by definition. It is absolutely pristine: there has never been a single allegation that we have got something wrong. We're not writing opinion pieces, though we do some-times write factual analysis, but the bulk of our publication is

---

262 Julian Assange, phone call with Yanis Varoufakis, March 24, 2020, https://www.yanisvaroufakis.eu/2020/03/24/last-night-julian-assange-called-me-here-is-what-we-talked-about/.

raw source material that cannot be attacked as something that has our editorial influence in it. So the only way to attack it becomes, in fact, through an ad hominem attack on the message. It's a very difficult position to be in, but since I'm already in it, I may as well keep the heat on me, and spare the other members of the organization."[263]

BRINGING KNOWLEDGE TO WHERE IT CAN DO GOOD

"The truth needs no policy position, so there does not need to be an intent. We have a framework, and the framework has an intent. We have policies that have an intent as a whole. And our intent is to bring knowledge to the people where it can do some good. We have, unlike every other media organization, a very concise and clear editorial policy. So our editorial policy is we accept information of diplomatic, political, ethical, or

---

263 Obrist, "In Conversation with Julian Assange, Part II," Hans Ulrich Obrist, Journal #26, e-flux, June 2011, https://www.e-flux.com/journal/26/67921/in-conversation-with-julian-assange-part-ii/.

historical significance that is under active suppression, that has not been published before."[264]

A PROUD RECORD

"We have a harm-minimization procedure. A harm-minimization procedure is that we don't want innocent people who have a decent chance of being hurt to be hurt. Now, no one has been hurt. There is no allegation by the Pentagon or any other official source that anyone has been physically harmed as a result of our publication of the Afghan War Logs, the Iraq War Diaries or the State Department records, or the 'Collateral Murder' video, or in fact anything we have done over the past four years in over 120 countries. Now, we are dealing with very significant and substantial information. There may come a time where in order to save people from war, to save people from corruption, to assist in taking a dictatorship to a democracy, that people incidentally come to harm. That is never our intention. That day may yet come, but that day has not come yet. And that is, in fact, a proud record for this organization."[265]

---

264 "WikiSecrets," interview by Martin Smith, PBS Frontline, documentary aired May 24, 2011, https://wikileaks.org/WikiSecrets-JulianAssange-Full.html.

265 Ibid.

EXPANDING THE INTELLECTUAL RECORD

"There are really two fundamental justifications [for what we're doing]. First of all, human civilization, its good part, is based upon our full intellectual record, and our intellectual record should be as large as possible if humanity is to be as advanced as possible. The second is that, in practice, releasing information is positive to those engaged in acts that the public supports and negative to those engaged in acts that the public does not support."[266]

NEVER GOTTEN IT WRONG

"WikiLeaks has been publishing for ten years. In that ten years we've published 10 million documents, several thousand individual publications, several thousand different sources. And we have never got it wrong."[267]

---

266 Assange, *When Google Met WikiLeaks,* p. 134.

267 "Secret World of U.S. Election."

Julian Assange is the founder and publisher of WikiLeaks and the author of *When Google Met WikiLeaks* (OR Books, 2014) and *Cypherpunks: Freedom and the Future of the Internet* (OR Books, 2012). Julian has won many awards for his journalism including the Amnesty International UK Media Award, Economist Award, Martha Gellhorn Prize for Journalism, Sydney Peace Foundation Prize, Walkley Award and many more.

Articles by Julian Assange have been published in the *New York Times*, the *Washington Post*, *Newsweek*, and *the Guardian*. Nominated for the Nobel Peace Prize on numerous occasions, his work as a journalist and publisher, and as a campaigner for freedom of expression, has been recognized at the highest level.

Julian is currently facing a 175 year sentence if extradited to the U.S. for his work as a publisher.

Karen Sharpe lives in Paris and has worked as a university teacher, journalist, writer, and editor.